THE POWER OF
WOMEN

ROMA SEN

TRUE SIGN
PUBLISHING HOUSE

Published by True Sign Publishing House

Address: SY. No. 21/2 & 21/3, Sonnenahalli,
Krishnarajapura, Bengaluru,
Karnataka - 560049 India
E-mail: truesignbooks@gmail.com
Website: www.truesign.in

The Power of Women

Author: Roma Sen

ISBN: 978-93-5584-971-7

First Edition: 2023

CONTENTS

The Power of Women

"The whole world is from her only, some pamper her like a mother and some are lovely like a sister."

"Don't consider a girl as a burden, she illuminates the name of not only the house but also the country, as soft as she is, she is equally tough, sometimes Kalpana Chawla illuminates her name, sometimes she fights like Rani Lakshmi Bai."

"A women walks on thorns even then she does not stop, even if troubles fall like a mountain, she does not bow down, she is the pride of her father, she is the life of her mother's heart."

Women as an important part of society cannot be imagined. There are many qualities like tolerance, patience, love and affection inside a woman which is the real power of a woman. If a woman decides to do something, she does not back down without completing that work.

Since ancient times, there have been many women in our society like Rani of Jhansi, Kalpana Chawla and Indira Gandhi, who have introduced women power from time to time and told the world that women are not weak but strong. Even in modern times, women have learned about their rights and have started taking decisions related to their lives on their own. Even today the woman is soft and sweet but she has awakened the feminine power within her and has started opposing injustice.

Today, even though woman has become aware and has recognized her confidence and willpower, still she is not safe . Even today women are considered weak and helpless. Men should respect women and do not oppress them so much that their tolerance ends and it takes the form of power, because whenever the patience of a woman is broken, then there is a holocaust. A woman is a divine form, therefore, women's power is heavy on all.

In the present times, along with being a capable housewife, women are also helpful and motivators of men in all fields of politics, religion, law, justice; Not only has the respect of modern women gone up in the society, but also the prestige has increased, the way women have registered their presence in the field of male monopoly like business and trade is commendable.

We should salute women power and help them in future because if the women of our country develop then every house, every street and the whole country will develop.

Never Underestimate the Power of a Women

"Never underestimate the power of a woman." This slogan, created by an advertising agency to promote **Ladies' Home Journal** in 1941, helped sell magazines because women were considered as economic powerhouses. Seventy six years later and we are still undervaluing women as a powerful force in the global economy. Even worse, we are underestimating how much more they could achieve if society finally had their back.

Today, on **International Women's Day**, women across the globe are coming together to show the depth of their power, and not just in the streets – they're showing it with their pocket books. Following the origin of International Women's Day, this year's global undertaking is boldly billed as "A Day Without a Woman." But what does a day without a woman mean for communities, societies, and economies?

Because women are powerful

Women are producers, consumers, and innovators. They are resourceful economic agents, proving every day that they can succeed, often in the face of persistent gender barriers. "A Day Without a Woman" means fewer women working to keep the production and service industry up; fewer women taking care of children, the elderly and all of us; fewer women spending money on goods that drive our economy. Simply put, when women don't work, the economy and society don't either.

Consider the following:

➢ A reduction in the gap between women's and men's labour force participation – or an increase in female labour force participation – results in **faster economic growth**.

➢ Women control, **70-80% of all consumer purchasing**.

➢ Women perform **two to ten times** more daily unpaid work by cooking, cleaning, and caring for family members. That is why men in virtually every country have more time for leisure activities, while women have less time for jobs and political participation.

> Women do all of this in spite of salaries, laws, and gender norms that continue to sell them short. In addition to unpaid work, no country has yet to achieve gender equality or equal pay for equal formal work. **Ninety per cent of countries** still have at least one law restricting women's economic opportunity. Gender stereotypes in the workplace mean that women are expected to be more helpful, to the point where men are **significantly more likely** to be recommended for promotions and raises than women who provide the same amount of help. If women closed their wallets, the consumer industry could grind to a halt.

Lucky for us, we already know the answer: Invest in girls and women

It is time to mainstream women's economic empowerment as a core component of thriving economies. If women and men participated equally in the formal economy, we would see $28 trillion added to annual GDP by 2014 – roughly the size of the U.S. and Chinese economies combined.

An investment in women's economic empowerment is also an investment in the entire community. Women are more likely than men to reinvest whatever time and money they have into their families, and their children's health and education in particular. The health, education, and social service industries collapse without women's participation. It is women who consistently pick up the invisible but essential tasks that keep the gears turning – from mentoring staff to administration work. And teams with greater gender diversity arrive at quicker, more creative solutions.

Women Deliver was one of the first civil society organizations to make the investment case for girls and women. That's because the data speaks for itself: when you invest in girls and women, it creates a powerful ripple effect that goes way beyond the individual – it powers progress for all.

The scope and impact of "A Day Without a Woman" strike is not yet known. But it is already clear that women wield significant economic power. Women are not, in fact, vulnerable victims, but committed change-makes, capable of powering economies and driving progress. We simply cannot afford to continue underestimating women's economic power. As we like to say, women deliver, and so much more than babies. It is urgent that we, in turn, deliver for them.

"A strong woman knows she has strength enough for the journey, but a woman of strength knows it is in the journey where she will become strong."

The Role of Women in Agriculture

The International Development Community has recognized that agriculture is an engine of growth and poverty reduction in countries where it is the main occupation of the poor. But the agriculture sector in many developing countries is under performing, in part because women, who represent a crucial resource in agriculture and the rural economy through their roles as farmers, labourers and entrepreneurs, almost everywhere face more severe constraints than men in access to productive resources. Efforts by national governments and the international community to achieve their goals for agricultural development, economic growth and food security will be strengthened and accelerated if they build on the contributions that women make and take steps to alleviate these constraints.

Women make essential contribution to the agricultural and rural economies in all developing countries. Their roles vary considerably between and within regions and are changing rapidly in many parts of the world, where economic and social forces are transforming the agricultural sector. Rural women often manage complex households and pursue multiple livelihood strategies. Their activities typically include producing agricultural crops, tending animals, processing and preparing food, working for wages in agricultural or other rural enterprises, collecting fuel and water, engaging in trade and marketing, caring for family members and maintaining their homes. Many of these activities are not defined as "economically active employment" in national accounts but they are essential to the well being of rural households. This paper contributes to the gender debate in agriculture by assessing the empirical evidence in three areas that has received much attention in literature.

- How much of the agricultural labour in the developing world is performed by women?

- What share of the world's food is produced by women?

- Do women face discrimination in rural labour markets?

What Women do in Agriculture and Rural Employment?

Women make important contribution of the rural economies of all regions of the world. However, the exact contribution both in terms of magnitude and its nature is often difficult to assess and shows a high degree of variation across countries and regions. This paper presents an overview of the evidence on the roles of women in agriculture and in rural labour markets. It also looks at demographic trends in rural areas with regard to the gender composition of rural populations.

Women in the agricultural labour force

Two types of data can contribute to measuring the contribution of women in the agricultural labour forces: statistics on the share of women in their economically active population in agriculture and time use surveys, which document the time spent by men and women in different activities.

Economically active population in agriculture

Data on the economically active population in agriculture are available for many countries, and provide the most comprehensive measure of the participation of women in agriculture.

In this measure, an individual is reported as being in the agricultural labour if he or she, underestimate female participation in agriculture for reasons discussed below, and caution is advised in interpreting changes over time because improvement in data collection may be responsible for some of the observed changes.

Figure I report weighted averages for the share of women in the agricultural labour force (or economically active in agriculture) in 5 major regions of the world.

According to these data, women comprise just over 40 per cent of the agricultural labour force in the developing world, a figure that has risen slightly since 1980 and ranges from about 20 per cent in the Americas to almost 50 per cent in Africa.

Even considering these data as lower bounds for the participation of women in the agricultural labour force, they do not support estimates above 60 per cent except for a few countries.

The global average is dominated by Asia, the sub-regional averages range from about 35 per cent in South Asia to almost 50 per cent in East and Southeast Asia.

The Asian average is dominated by China, where the female share of the agricultural labour force has increased slightly during the past three decades.

The female share in India has remained steady at just over 30 per cent. These very large countries make changes in some smaller countries where the female share of the agricultural labour force appear to have increased dramatically, now exceeding 50 per cent in Bangladesh. Other Asian countries such as Malaysia have seen declining female labour shares in agriculture. Women make up almost 50 per cent of the agricultural labour force in sub-Saharan Africa, an increase from about 45 per cent in 1980. The averages in Africa range from just over 40 per cent in Southern Africa to just over 50 per cent in Eastern Africa.

These sub-regional averages have remained fairly stable since 1980, with the exception of Northern Africa, where the female share appears to have risen from 30 per cent to almost 45 per cent.

The sub-regional data for Africa conceal wide differences between countries both in the share of female labour in agriculture and the rising trend. The developing countries of the American have much lower average female agricultural labour shares than the other developing country regions at just over 20 per cent in 2010, slightly higher than in 1980. The South American countries of Bolivia, Brazil, Colombia, Ecuador and Peru dominate the average and are responsible for most of the rising trend.

Figure 2 shows that agriculture is relative to manufacturing and services, the most important source of employment for women by a wide margin in South Asia and in sub-Saharan Africa. It is also the most important sector for women in East Asia and South-East Asia but nearly equally so with services.

Agriculture is much more important for women than for men in terms of employment in South Asia and the Middle East. It is somewhat more important for women than for men in East Asia, North Africa and sub-Saharan Africa. In Central and South Eastern Europe and in Latin America women are much more concentrated in the service sector. The figure shows that both the level of employment and the distribution of employment in different sectors vary substantially across regions.

However, there is always a significant gap between the level of male and female employment and for women the service and/or agriculture sectors are relatively more important than the manufacturing sector.

Many researchers have questioned the gender patterns that emerge from the employment data presented here and above (see for example Beneria, 1981). Deere (2005) identifies a number of potential sources of underestimation of female employment in labour markets, and in agriculture in particular.

She notes that rural women in Latin America are likely to reply that "their home" is their primary responsibility, even if they are heavily engaged in agriculture. Other difficulties arise because censuses tend to emphasize income-generating activities – therefore, underestimating subsistence production – and because agricultural production is often defined as fieldwork. Activities such as rearing small livestock, kitchen gardening, and post-harvest processing are often under counted. Deere focuses on critiquing the numbers for Latin America, but similar criticism are also valid for other regions, like South Asia.

Time spent in agricultural activities

Time use surveys attempt to provide a more complete account of time use by men and women than are available from the labour force statistics reported above. Such studies usually are not nationally representative and are not directly comparable because they usually cover small samples, report on different types of activities (that are not always clearly specified) and use different methodologies. Despite these caveats, a summary of the evidence from studies which specify time use by agricultural activity suggests interesting patterns.

Time-use surveys that cover all agricultural activities reveal considerable variation across countries, and sometimes within countries, but the data are broadly similar to the labour force statistics discussed above. In Africa, estimate of the time contribution of women to agricultural activities ranges from about 30 per cent in the Gambia to 60-80 per cent in different parts of Cameroon.

In Asia, estimates range from 32 per cent in India to over 50 per cent in China. The range is lower in Latin America, but exceeds 30 per cent in some parts of Peru.

Two separate studies are reported each for Zambia and Peru, and differences reflect different time periods and locations within the countries.

A striking degree of within country variation is shown by time use data for India. While the nationally representative data indicates that the national average for women's share of total time use in agriculture is 32 per cent, data for West Bengal and Rajasthan reports women's share as less than 10 per cent to more than 40 per cent, respectively. But in both areas, younger women contribute a higher share of the total time provided in agriculture by their age group than older women do in theirs. In Rajasthan, for example, girls between 14 and 19 years of age contribute up to 60 per cent of the total time spent on agriculture by their age group (Jain, 1996).

Time-use studies also reveal that female time use in agriculture varies widely depending on the crop and the phase of the production cycle, the age and ethnic group in question, the type of activity and other factors. Data from Indonesia reveals greater involvement of women in upland rice than wet rice and in the management of young plantation crops such as cinnamon and rubber rather than the same crops at maturity.

Time-use studies also reveal that female time-use in agriculture can also vary widely within one country, depending on the crop, the technology and other factors.

Time-use studies permit a rich analysis of what men and women do in agriculture and how their roles may differ by crop, location, management structure, age and ethnic group.

They offer policy relevant information about where, when and how to target interventions aimed at women and how to bring men into the process constructively.

Given the variability in gender roles in agriculture, generalizations about time-use from one region to another are not appropriate. Studies that consider the gender roles within their specific geographic and cultural context can provide practical guidance for policy makers and practitioners involved in technology investments, extension services, post-harvest activities and marketing intervention.

A few of the time-use studies present the precise breakdown of time-use by farming activity. Five of the studies, covering six cases, have information on five common categories: land preparation, fertilizer application, weeding, harvesting and storage.

All studies with the exception of Bangladesh (where, for rice, women's time is entirely spent on post-harvest activities) found weeding to be a predominantly female activity, followed by harvesting and fertilizer application.

Women were typically involved in all other activities but did not provide a majority of labour.

Finally, we note that the time-use studies that collected the relevant data confirm the popular perception that women overwhelmingly provide the greatest proportion of household time spent on food processing and preparation. If these aspects of food preparation are included, women's labour share could well exceed to 60 per cent in many African countries and could approach 60 per cent in many Asian ones.

Women's contribution to agricultural production

As seen above, women play a significant role in the agricultural labour force and in agricultural activities, although to a varying degree.

Consequently their contribution to agricultural output is undoubtedly extremely significant, although difficult to qualify with any accuracy. It has often been claimed that women produce 60-80 per cent of food. However, assigning contributions to agricultural outputs by gender is problematic because in most agricultural households both men and women are involved in crop production.

It can be attempted to allocate output by gender by assuming that specific crops are grown by women and others by men and then aggregating the value of women's and men's crops to determine the share grown by women. Researchers have occasionally used this approach, especially in West Africa, where there are distinguishable cropping patterns by gender.

Yet, a careful analysis of agriculture in Ghana finds that while there are gendered patterns of cropping, the distinctions between men's and women's crops do not hold up well enough to use them to make inferences about men's and women's relative contribution to production.

In addition, gendered patterns of cropping may change over time (Doss, 2022).

A direct comparison of production is possible between male and female headed households, but since the latter tend to have smaller farms and use fewer purchased inputs their output is naturally smaller.

Female-headed households represent between 3 and 38 per cent of all households and produce between 2 and 17 per cent of the value of food produced.

These data suggest that female-headed households produce less than their share would predict if resources use and productivity were equal with male-headed households.

In reality, in most situations, the question of women's contribution to agricultural and food production cannot be answered with any degree of accuracy. Women do not usually produce food separately from men. Most food is produced with labour contributions of both men and women in a collaborative process.

Quantifying the share of food produced by women involves making arbitrary assumptions about gender roles in the production process, which are not likely to hold universally. For example, if men typically provide the labour to clear the field and women plant and weed the crops, both men and women are involved in harvesting. In these and other similar cases it becomes impossible to separate output by gender.

Nonetheless, all the indirect evidence presented above in terms of labour participation and output by varying definitions of gender indicates that it is unlikely that women produce as much as 60-80 per cent of the food in developing countries. Women play a fundamental role in all the stages of the food cycle in all regions, but these roles differ by region. Taking account of the heterogeneity of their contribution is essential if policies and interventions are to be effective.

Women as livestock keepers

Within pastoralist and mixed farming systems, livestock play an important role in supporting women and in improving their financial situation and women are heavily engaged in this sector. An estimated two-thirds of poor livestock keepers, totaling approximately 400 million people, are women.

They share responsibility with men and children for the care of animals, and particular species and types of activity are more associated with women than men.

For example, women often have a prominent role in managing poultry and dairy animals and in caring for other animals that are housed and fed within the homestead.

When tasks are divided, men are more likely to be involved in constructing housing and herding of grazing animals and in marketing of products if women's mobility is constrained. The influence of women is strong in the use of eggs, milk and poultry meat for home consumption and they often have control over marketing and the income from these products.

Perhaps for this reason poultry and small scale dairy projects have been popular investments for development projects aiming to improve the lot of rural women. In some countries small-scale pig production is also dominated by women.

Female-headed households are as successful as male-headed households in generating income from their animals, although they tend to own smaller numbers of animals, probably because of labour constraints.

Ownership of livestock is particularly attractive to women in societies where access to land is restricted to men. While the role of women in small-scale livestock production is well recognized, much less has been documented about the engagement of women in intensive production and the market chains associated with large commercial enterprises.

Demand for livestock products has grown much faster than the demand for crop staples during the past 40 years, fueled by rising incomes, particularly in Asia and Latin America, and this trend is expected to continue.

While pastoralist and small-scale mixed farming systems continue to be important in meeting the needs of rural consumers, the demands of growing urban populations are increasingly supplied with meat, milk and eggs from intensive commercial systems. The has important implications for the engagement of women in the livestock sector because of the different roles, responsibilities and access to resources that are evident within different scales of production system and at different points on the production and marketing chain.

The available evidence suggests that the role of women in meeting these changing demands may diminish, for two reasons. The first is that when livestock enterprises scale up, the control of decisions and income and sometimes of the entire enterprise often shifts to men.

This is not a universal phenomenon – for example, in Vietnam, many medium-sized duck-breeding enterprises are managed by women – but it is common and can be explained by the limited access that women have to land and credit. The second important factor is that all smallholders face challenges when the livestock sector intensifies and concentrates and many go out of business.

This is particularly evident for pig and poultry owners but not confined to those species. Given the more limited ability of women to start their own businesses, this implies that they will tend to become employees rather than self-employed.

In specialized activities like production of day-old chicks, in the provision of services, and in slaughtering, processing and retail, women are visible wherever painstaking semi-skilled work is to be done, but very little information is available about the extent of their involvement as compared to that of men, or their control over resources.

Women in fisheries and aquaculture

Nearly 45 million people world-wide were directly engaged, full-time or part-time, in the fishery primary sector. In addition, about 135 million people are estimated to be employed in the secondary sector, including post-harvest activities.

While comprehensive data are not available on a basis, case studies suggest that women may comprise up to 30 per cent of the total employment in fisheries, including primary and secondary activities.

Women have rarely engaged in commercial offshore and long distance capture fisheries because of the vigorous work involved but also because of women's domestic responsibilities and/or social norms. Women are more commonly occupied in subsistence and commercial fishing from small boats and canoes in coastal or inland waters.

Women also contribute as entrepreneurs and provide labour before, during and after the catch in both artisanal and commercial fisheries. Studies of women in aquaculture, especially in Asia where aquaculture has a long tradition, indicate that the contribution of women in labour is often greater than men although there is almost a complete absence of macro-level aquaculture-related data.

Women are reported to constitute 33 per cent of the rural aquaculture workforce in China, 42 per cent in Indonesia and 80 per cent in Vietnam.

The most significant role played by women in both artisanal and industrial fisheries is at the processing and marketing stags, where they are very active in all regions, in some countries, women have become important entrepreneurs in fish processing; in fact, most fish processing is performed by women, either in their own household-level industries or as wage labours in the large-scale processing industry.

Women and unpaid household responsibilities

Women are generally less able than men to participate in economic opportunities because they face a work burden that men do not.

In most societies, women are responsible for most of the household and child-rearing activities as well rearing of small livestock, although norms differ by culture and over time.

This additional work burden is unpaid and limits a women's capacity to engage in income-earning activities, which often require a minimum fixed time before being profitable. Furthermore, the nature of tasks, such as caring for children and elderly household members, requires women to stay near the home, thus limiting options to work for a wage.

Time scarcity forces many women to start-up cottage industries, such as handicrafts, which are often characterized by low returns and limited potential for expansion.

Gender differences become clearer when looking at women's workloads. It is estimated that women provide 85 to 90 per cent of the time spent on household food processing and preparation across a wide range of countries.

Women are also usually responsible for child-care and household chores, Depending on the household structure and size, these tasks may be extremely time intensive.

Time allocation studies have shown that women work significantly more than men if care-giving is included in the calculations. Sharma et al finds that girls do significantly more work in household chores and on the farm as compared to boys in Himachal Pradesh, India. Fontana and Natali find a marked gender bias in most unpaid work in Tanzania. Women, and in particular women from low-income groups and living in areas with limited facilities, spend long hours on water and fuel collection, food preparation and other domestic and child-care activities to compensate for poor infrastructure, shows that women are responsible for about 65 per cent of all transport activities in rural households including travel for firewood, water and transport to the grinding mill.

Due to the gender-specific assignment of tasks, any changes affecting the family or the environment often have different implications for men and women.

For example, it has caused a significant increase in the time needed to care for sick family members or the orphaned children of relatives. Deforestation leads women to collect firewood from increasingly further distances from the homestead. Fontana and Natali calculate that time-savings from unpaid-work reducing infrastructure for water collection and food preparation as equivalent to 66 thousand and 4,590 thousand full-time jobs, respectively.

Gender differences within rural labour markets

In addition to differences in male and female labour participation rates notes earlier, there are also major gender differences in employment patterns within labour markets for several reasons which hold across cultures and regions.

Most importantly, as a result of household and child-rearing, women are more likely to engage in self-employment activities rather than higher-paying wage employment. Due to child-care responsibilities economically active women often leave the labour market and thus accumulate less work experience. As a result of time constraints, women are also more likely to work in part time jobs and in informal arrangement that pay less and/or provides fewer benefits, but provide more flexibility.

Women are also more concentrated in certain phases or activities of the supply chain. Occupational segregation into low-technology occupations limits the opportunities to generate new skills and capabilities, thus hindering future professional development and reinforcing the discrimination towards these sectors as low-pay and low-status occupations.

Finally, there is a well documented pay gap in urban labour markets which are likely to exist in rural labour markets as well – in that women are paid less even for equivalent jobs and comparable levels of education and experience. Wage gaps between men and women have been further discussed below.

Frequently women are confined to working in particular sectors and in certain jobs, often as a result of their disadvantaged position with respect to human capital and bargaining power. On the basis of national level case studies in Latin America, Katz concludes that, within the non-farm sector, wage employment is almost universally dominated by men and self-employment by women. Furthermore, even when women find formal sector employment, they do not easily advance into managerial positions. In Colombia's flower cutting industry, for example, between 60 and 80 per cent of the unskilled workers are women, while they have a much lower share of managerial or professional jobs. Moreover, in sectors producing industries – women tend to be replaced by males, as profits increase.

Intra-household inequality can also weaken a woman's position outside of the home. Women are over represented in jobs characterized by low wages, high job insecurity and generally poor labour standards. When women have limited decision-making ability within the household or low access to resources and house hold income, they are most likely to accept lower wages. Kantor notes that, for most women in northern India, labour market participation is a survival strategy for the household, not a means of improving standards of living or voice in the household.

Evidence confirms that women tend to cluster in lower paying jobs. Hertz et al. 2009, explores the issue of job distribution according to pay in rural areas. They acknowledge that non-agricultural jobs tend to pay on average more than agricultural jobs. Based on this, they define three categories of jobs:

- Low wage jobs, which pay less than the median agricultural wage.

- Medium wage activities, which pay more than the median agriculture wage, but less than the median non-agricultural wage and

- High wage jobs, which pay more than the median non-agricultural wage. Applying this categorization to data from 14 countries form the RIGA database, reveals that in all countries, with the exception of Panama the distribution of women tends to be skewed much more than that of men towards lower paid jobs and non-agricultural activities.

Women also suffer from wage gaps, although data documenting this in rural settings is limited. Wage inequalities are typically contractual arrangements that differ for men and women, with women usually having worse conditions of employment, typically women receive lower wages for the same work.

Evidence from a sample of 14 countries shows that on average women are paid 28 per cent less than males in rural than in urban areas for half of the countries sampled.

While women continue to face occupational segregation and discrimination in rural labour markets, some new forms of organization in supply chains for exports oriented crops and agro-processing have created better paying employment opportunities for women in the packing stage of non-traditional agro export production and it may be one of the most impotent developments for female employment over the last few decades.

Women are clearly an important part of the agricultural labour force, but agriculture and agricultural value chains are equally important to women as a source of employment.

Commercial value chains for high value products such as fresh fruits, vegetable, flower and livestock products are growing rapidly to supply urban supermarkets and export markets. The growth of modern value chains and the broader structural transformation of the agricultural sector in many developing countries have major implications for women's employment, but the impact of these trends for women has received relatively little analytical attention.

Women dominate employment in many of the high value agricultural commodity chains in sub- Saharan Africa and Latin America. New jobs in exports oriented agro-industries may not employ men and women on equal terms, however, they often provide better opportunities for women that exist within the confines of traditional agriculture and can also be instruments of change with significant implications for women and rural development.

The flower industry in Latin America provides an interesting case in contrasting points of view. In Colombia, for example, Friedemann-Sanchez finds that 64 per cent of the workforce directly growing fresh cut flowers for export are women and consider this type of agro-industrial work skilled, while others consider it unskilled. While women do have supervisory jobs among those directly involved in cultivation activities, they have a much lower share of managerial or professional jobs in other aspects of the sector. Similarly, Fontana finds that in sectors producing primarily for the export market, women tend to be replaced by males as profits increase.

The arrival of the flower industry in the Ecuadorian town of Cayambe in the late 1980s affected time-use patterns in surprising ways. The total time spent by women in paid and unpaid work did not increase, contrary to a frequent criticism of agricultural export development which maintains that women are unduly burdened by work in the industry. Indeed, the most compelling evidence of the industry's impact was on men's increased participation in housework. In Cotocachi, Ecuador, in contrast, women were not prepared to move or even commute to work in the flower industry despite the higher wages offered there. The women did not view flower employment as an option, indicating either that their husbands would not allow them to work or that the work would be detrimental to family relations.

In Senegal, the growth of modern horticulture supply chains has been associated with direct beneficial effects for rural women and reduced gender inequalities in rural areas. That study also finds that women benefit more in high value smallholder contract farming in which they often provide unpaid family labour.

Small holder production systems in rapidly growing areas are facing increasing pressure to commercialize, diversify and expand. Increasing scales of production are being observed particularly in the livestock sector, which attempts to supply rapidly growing markets for meat, milk and eggs. Small scale producers face particular pressures as size and private health and safety standards set by large retailers and wholesale buyers become increasingly important.

Studies cited in Reardon and Berdegue show that, in general, farmers who produce for supermarkets are larger, more educated, have more access to information, are able to hire in labour, have greater access to irrigation and are closer to transport infrastructure.

Conclusion

In this paper, we collate the empirical evidence on women's roles in agriculture, setting the stage for subsequent analysis on gender differences in agriculture and the potential gains from removing these gender differences. The main findings are:

Women comprise about 43 percent of the global agricultural labour force and of that in developing countries, but this figure makes considerable variation across regions and within countries according to age and social class.

Women comprise half or more of the agricultural labour force in many African and Asian countries, but the share is much less in some.

Time-use surveys, which provide a more comprehensive assessment of how men and women spend their time, further emphasize the heterogeneity among countries and within countries in women's contribution to agriculture. The labour burden of rural women exceeds that of men, and includes a higher proportion of unpaid household responsibilities related to preparing food and collecting fuel and water.

The contribution of women to agricultural and food production is clearly significant. However, it is impossible to verify empirically the share produced by women because agriculture is usually a venture among household members and involves a range of resources and inputs that cannot be readily assigned by gender.

Women's participation in rural labour markets show much heterogeneity at the regional level, but women are over represented in unpaid, seasonal and part-time work, and the available evidence suggests that women are often paid less than men, for the same work. We conclude that accurate, current, regionally specific information and analysis is necessary for good gender-aware agricultural policy making. Data collection has improved substantially over the decades, as has our understanding of the complexity of women's roles and the need to collect data not only on primary activities but on all women's activities. Data are needed to better understand gender roles in agriculture and how they change over time response to new opportunities.

We have shown that women's roles are diverse and that they vary across regions and countries. These roles cannot be understood properly, and interventions targeting cannot be designed effectively, without also understanding their differential access to land, capital, assets, human capital, and other productive resources.

The Power of Women Coming Together

When women come together, change happens.

I think I've always known this intuitively, but I really started paying attention 15 years ago, when I visited a village in the foothills of the Himalayas. I spent most of my day with the village Chief, and I could tell he was giving me the "official" tour. Eventually, though, some of the women gave me their own tour they told me their kids were dying from diarrhea, so sanitation was their most important priority, but they couldn't get their Chief interested. Finally, after a lot of strategizing, they agreed to take a different tack. They convinced him that a toilet was a status symbol, so he finally bought one. Then they outsmarted him again by putting it right near his house, where they knew it would be kept clean.

This isn't just a story about cleverness, though these women were very clever. It's a story about the nature of progress. Sometimes, change comes from the top down. Other times, it comes from the bottom up, when ordinary people come together, think up extraordinary ideas, and insist on being heard.

We exercise power through the communities we create.

Women have always been masters of this kind of grassroots change. Because we've had to be, we don't always have equal access to formal authority – not yet – so we exercise power through the communities we create. Now, no matter where I visit, when I see women chatting around the well or girls sitting together in a high school cafeteria, I know there's often serious politics and movement-building happening.

The reason I decided to make access to contraceptives one of my top priorities is that I heard so many women around the world talking about how much it would change their lives if they could decide if and when to get pregnant. The stories they shared were so personal and so powerful that they shifted the way I thought about the work we were doing at the **Gates Foundation**. What started as informal conversations with women became my formal agenda. Women want the world to get better. For us, for everybody, that's our dream, and we mobilize each other to make those dreams come true.

"Some women fear the fire, some women simply become it..."

Harnessing the Power of Women: Building High-Perpormance Teams

The ways in which many women are working and living have changed drastically since the onset of the COVID-19 pandemic. According to new research by Deloitte Global, nearly 82% of women surveyed said their lives have been negatively disrupted by the pandemic, and nearly 70% of women who have experienced these disruptions are concerned about their ability to progress in their careers. Even before COVID struck, the trend of women dropping out of the workforce due to various reasons, most predominant being the inability to balance demands of home and workplace was worrisome. While most organizations recognize that it is a huge waste of talent and a drain on the nation financially, not much is being done about it.

In a webcast in collaboration with the Momenta Group, **Neelam Dhawan**, Director ICICI Bank, Anita S Guha, Talent Advisor-Chief Information Office, IBM India, and **Swami Swaminathan**, Resident Director Momenta, delved into what measures can be taken by organizations to arrest this trend, leveraging flexible and virtual teams to harness the power of women in building a high performing global workforce for tomorrow and the role which futuristic talent models can play in building high-performance teams.

Leveraging flexi and futuristic talent deployment models for harnessing the power of women

While it has been an unprecedented and challenging year, Swami shared that still there is a silver lining to it given the fact it was also a year of innovation and a huge paradigm shift towards flexible working hours - something that was unimaginable 15 years back. What has become clear is that the only certainty that will be sought is flexibility in everything. The year has made smart managers roll out flexible talent deployment models based on customer demand.

Consider this - over 50% increase in flexible staffing solutions was implemented by businesses this year. The year has also enabled employees to select flexible working hours to meet their work-life balance.

Swami believes that the year 2020 has been a year of pervasive technology adoption. Technology is enabling organizations to create world-class teams by playing a huge role in managing flexibility. There is no rigidity in talent management today and companies can tap the global talent pool to choose from as required. Hence today, organizations can create world-class teams by leveraging technology to bring onboard millions of talented women, demolish rigidity in the talent space that has been around hiring women, and build flexible high-performance virtual teams as needed-at the right time, at the right place, and the right price.

Ultimately, the new mantra in times ahead will be flexibility and agile, flexible working model such as that of Momenta's, which will not only harness the immense talent of women but also build and deliver a workforce of the future where women have a platform to thrive.

COVID-19 has affected women disproportionately

Taking the conversation further, Anita reiterated that COVID-19 has affected women disproportionately as many of the industries affected by COVID are female-dominated such as airlines, hospitality and retail. Secondly, the nature of women's work as compared to men's work tends to be more precarious as their proportion is higher in part-time or contractual jobs. Thirdly, in terms of responsibilities, women share a greater responsibility for child-care, elder care, and home care in addition to their work responsibilities. And these have become exacerbated in the times of the pandemic.

So in these circumstances, what can organizations do? First, they need to recognize those serious diversity implications which are not short-term. They need to educate leaders so that they are not biased. They also need to reinforce initiatives to attract, develop and retain talent, provide ups- killing/ reskilling opportunities, look at employee assistance programs and extend protection to gig workers as they will include a large number of women. On an individual level, Anita shared that individuals need to build resilience be it men or women. Individuals need to look at building resilience in holistic terms-in mind, body and spirit. One important aspect of this is networking.

Individuals need to build diverse networks during this period not in terms of gender diversity but also in terms of organizational and economic strata as well. They also need to increase the depth and the breadth of their skills and aim at developing multiple specializations.

"Behind every successful woman is a tribe of other successful woman who have her back."

The Power of Women at Work (POWW)

Embracing Power and Possibilities

The ELC recognizes the remarkable responsibility Black Women have to navigate their social and work lives in the face of adversity and bias. Stereotypes of the angry Black Woman, the militant Black Woman, and the Black Superwoman all serve the same function: to reduce the professional Black Woman to a single story – and by doing so, to reduce her power.

At the ELC, it is easy for us to reject these classic and pejorative tropes, because we know the full story: one where the real power of Black Women at work is a healing balm, a discerning spirit, and an uplifting energy. We don't accept traditional notions of power which focus on the ability to compel others to do what we want. Instead, we re-imagine power as the ability to be the best and fullest version of yourself in whatever spaces you occupy. And we have created a professional development experience appropriate for this more expansive definition of the power we know all Black Women have. Imagine a training event where you are encouraged to re-imagine how the power of women is defined and expressed. Participate in sessions like:

- **Make it, Break it, or Leave it** – Learn when and how to apply your power to improve your current work situation, fundamentally disrupt it, or transition to another opportunity entirely.

- **Am I frightening…or are you just frightened?** – Discover the strategies and tactics to manage relationships with individuals, groups and organizations who might not be ready to accept a Black Woman who claims and exercises her full power.

- **Tactical Analysis** – Deconstruct the 5+ most common tropes applied to Black Women at work in order to more fully understand the gains and losses of using each as you move through your corporate journey.

The Power of Women at Work is a one-day symposium designed to equip Black professionals with the strategies, tactics and inspiration they need to re-imagine their career journey and accelerate their progress towards their goals. The candid conversations, game-changing solutions, insightful panels, networking, and partnering opportunities will keep you engaged. Register now because you do not want to miss this amazing opportunity!

You don't have to do it alone. Join as at the **2022 Power of Women and Work**…and embrace your power and explore possibility.

Here's what to expect:

- Discover how to accelerate your success in the workplace by managing your emotions and enhancing your well-being.

- Reach across the aisle to hear from men in the movement combating gender and racial equity in the workplace.

- Discover the right way to tell your story and own your voice.

- Use proven negotiation strategies to create an ideal and sustainable work environment from flexible work location and delivery to advocating for work life balance.

- Learn how to move from burnout to blaze, dealing with the emotional toll of race and gender bias.

- Network with women looking to partner and create your circle.

Objectives

During this program participants will:

- Expand self and organizational awareness to enhance building coalitions that drive change.

- Explore creativity, ingenuity and leadership of Black Women.

- Identify ways to forecast and predict the future of work using artificial intelligence(AI) and technology.

- Practice techniques to lead from a position of power to accelerate pipeline development for themselves and others.

"A strong woman will automatically stop trying if she feels unwanted. She won't fix it or beg, she'll just walk away."

The Power of Women in Family Business

Encouraging studies have examined women's changing roles over the years. However, studies that examine the role of women in family businesses are sparse and fragmented. Various scholars have indicated the need for more systematic and extensive research into the factors that are affecting women's involvement, leadership and performance in family businesses.

This was an important area of focus in the **Step 2019 Global Family Business** survey, and the in- depth interviews with prominent female and male family business leaders that followed. Based on the conversations that took place, **"The Power of Women in Family Business: A Generational Shift in Purpose and Influence"** takes an up-close look at the demographic shifts that are changing the role of women in family businesses, the value that women contribute, the various forms of influence they have and the unique competitive advantages they can deliver.

Changing demographics are creating new roles and leadership opportunities for women in family businesses. Alongside these opportunities, external factors such as societal prejudice, unconscious gender bias and family traditions are examined, as well as stereotypes that need to be challenged to provide a road map for women family business leaders of the future.

The Hidden CEO

Due to the influence of societal bias in the past, as well as cultural or family traditions in some cases, women ere consciously or inadvertently consigned to the role of 'chief emotional officer' in some family business situations. In this 'hidden' CEO role, they took care of the emotional needs of the family, keeping the family together and perpetuating the family's values and traditions.

The segregation of roles based on gender, both at home and in business, can be traced back to the Industrial Revolution. While men were associated with traits such as independence, autonomy, success and achievement, women were generally classified as nurturing and caring. Some of this gender bias continues today, even when it isn't conscious.

Traditionally feminine characteristics such as loyalty, concern, sensitivity to the needs of others, problem-solving and conflict resolution genuinely reflect a holistic leadership style – for women and men, in a family business, these unique characteristics and the associated management style are assets to both the family and the business, combining loyalty to the firm and family with a sensitivity to individuals' need and a decision-making process that is based on instinct and institution as well as evidence.

This is a constructive approach for any business and can create a potential competitive advantage in family businesses in particular.

How women are redefining 'women's work'?

Industries that have traditionally been dominated by men are inclined to exhibit more gender bias than others. In such cases, women are encouraged to go into traditional 'women's job's', and their ability to be leaders of these businesses may not be well recognized.

Nevertheless, despite a conventional view of 'women's work' in some parts of the world and in certain industries, a brighter light is shining through the glass ceiling of many family businesses. In what would have been considered a non-traditional female occupation in the past, particularly in male-dominated industries such as heavy manufacturing, an increasing number of highly competent women leaders are now standing confidently in the limelight.

Several of the women in family business who contributed their views to the article are founders and co-founders of companies in industries that would historically be labeled as 'men's work', including steel and scrap metal processing, cement manufacturing and the production of hardware products. Their view is that there should not be a bias towards women or men in any business; that diverse ideas and experiences add tremendous value to a team, making it more interesting and generating higher levels of innovation.

Many of these female family business leaders are successfully breaking down the barriers and redefining how some women in family businesses may have been perceived in the past. They are not waiting for some other person or some other time for the environment to change around them.

While biases may persist in some parts of the world, industries and even among some families, the interviews have shown that the role of women in family business is changing and will likely escalate as a new generation of successors assume the business reins.

The transformational power of women

It has generally been held that women, by their nature, encourage more collaboration and consultation than their male counterparts. The women interviewed agreed with that view. Through the generations, many have been raised to be more sensitive to the needs of others and more social as mother, peacekeeper and caretaker.

Nevertheless, the female family business leaders interviewed raised a concern regarding women who are expected to have this naturally enhanced level of sensitivity and face the danger of being pigeon holed as the chief emotional officer of the family business – and nothing more. When this is the case, there is a danger that female family members will not be socialized and groomed to internalize the business values and practices to the same extent as their male family members. And by not being given the same opportunities to actively participate in the business and build their own successful careers, they risk being left out of opportunities to assume leadership positions.

Family businesses led by female CEOs generally have a distinct transformational and less autocratic approach to leadership, as we observed in the transformational leadership style of many of the family business leaders with whom we spoke. The evidence generally shows that women tend to encourage individuals and teams to pursue new business opportunities, identify opportunities for change and make decisions on their own.

Succession by merit

As highlighted in our first article in this series regarding the topic of succession, **"The courage to choose wisely,"** traditional family firms have often followed the implicit rule of primogeniture in matters of succession and inheritance – transferring the business from the father to the first born child and often the first born son. To prepare them for their future roles, sons have often been socialized around the family business during dinner table conversations at home and some early involvement in the activities of the business.

Sons and daughters often have different experiences in this socialization process, however. In particular, daughters can be heavily influenced by the family's traditional gender roles, which are formed at a young age during regular interactions with the family. It is these types of experiences that may lead female family members to be more concerned about the family and its needs, than the needs of the family firm when primogeniture is the preferred succession model and they are not provided with the same opportunities for career growth as those of their male siblings.

However, the sentiment gathered from the conversations that took place is that change is in the wind in many countries across the globe with merit increasingly becoming the primary criteria for choosing the right successor.

The interviews with family business leaders have shown that even though primogeniture is still the norm for succession in many countries, as well as in individual family business, new rules in certain countries are opening up leadership opportunities for women in family firms. One important example is that of China, where the gender equality movement has raised the social status of women and the one-child policy has given women equal access to resources.

Further change is on the horizon, with improved access to higher levels of education coupled with shrinking family size, and the **Step 2019 Global Family Business** survey shows that the role of women in family business is continuing in progress.

The impact of societal change on family business leadership

To respond to the mounting need to address the issue of under representation of women in top management positions, new national and cultural norms that advance the roles of women in family business are emerging.

As an example, in the last 2 decades, women's visibility in Venezuelan family firms has been favourably influenced by their greater involvement in the labour market. Many young women successors to Venezuelan family businesses have shown that they can take charge of their businesses just as effectively as their male counterparts.

Such is the case in the Visani family, owners of Venezuela's **Inversora Lockey C.A**, where the founder included his daughters in the family business from an early age – even though the family's companies operated in what would be considered to be traditionally male industries.

A challenge to outdated mindsets

Although the family business legacy may be handed down to them, women around the world continue to play multiple roles in the business as well as the family, and often shoulder the primary responsibility for the care of children and the household.

Some continue to face the challenge of needing to prove their "legitimacy' as leaders; to prove their mettle and succeed in managing and leading their business.

As with women in non-family businesses, women in family firms require strong networks that are not dominated by family influence as well as mentoring and guidance to orient them successfully towards management and leadership roles.

For young female family leaders, acknowledging and celebrating the efforts of generations of women who have preceded them is viewed as important.

Women supporting women is more prevalent in the younger generations because of this mindset and a strong commitment for women to empower each other.

This is the way things should be for women in business, and family business leaders interviewed noted the importance of acknowledging that this level of support isn't the way it has always been.

It's the hard work of countless numbers of women and men who have come before that has helped to open the door for a new generation of female leaders.

Gaining a fresh perspective on family business leadership

Women and men have an opportunity to strengthen their family business by embracing their difference and not fighting against them.

Family businesses that are committed to empowering women might start by evaluating their beliefs and perceptions and encouraging open discussions of everyone's viewpoints within the family, especially those among different generation and genders, even if those conversations may be uncomfortable at first.

The courage to be candid and open to a new perspective has the power to change an existing and likely outdated narrative regarding the roles that women play in family business and the competitive advantage that they can contribute in the future.

The good news is that women in family business are strategically placed to bring about this change in their own companies and in society at large – as role models and guides for the next-generation women who will contribute to the future talent pool.

A diversity of views and approaches has tremendous power in helping to move family business towards more interesting and prosperous futures. Greater diversity also harnesses the resilience and adaptability that are the hallmarks of family businesses and as leading voices at the forefront of change.

Welcome to River-Empowerment

River – The Power of Women is purely a trust-oriented concern which help the women in creating awareness and encouraging them to develop their businesses on their own and make them successful in their life, The main objective of our concern is to empower poor women working in the informal sector and to organize self-employed strategies for women.

It is represented by its FOUNDER TRUSTEE and they shall have powers to represent the trust in all matters relating to the trust. They also raise global awareness on women begging in India. We join hands with the women of India to promote and provide justice to all women especially the poor and needy.

Business Opportunities –

•	Each woman is different, and so are their needs. RIVER analyzes these needs and provides them support with business solutions.

•	Some of our RIVER women display their talents and the products speak for themselves.

•	By supplying: Catering Service Stationery and Printing Materials, Gift Articles, Cleaning Items, etc.

•	Education: train them on Beauty, Bakery, Car and Auto driving, Tailoring and Embroidery, Mobile service, etc...

•	By outsourcing: House Keeping services, Canteen, Security, Lift, Valet Services, etc...

"The most alluring thing a woman can have is confidence."

The World's Most Powerful Women

Vladimir Putin's unprovoked invasion of Ukraine was a defining moment for Europe. The European Commission President, Ursula von der Leyen rose to the challenge. A week after the war began, she announced three major economic sanctions against Russia – banning transactions with its central bank, closing airspace to Russian plane travel and barring Kremlin-owned news agencies.

"Protecting our liberty comes at a price," von der Leyen said. "This is our principle: freedom is priceless." For her leadership during the Ukraine war, as well as her handling of the Covid-19 pandemic, von der Leyen sits atop the 19th annual Forbes list of the World's Most Powerful Women.

Her influence is unique – no one else on the list formulates policy on behalf of 450 million people – but her commitment to a free and democratic society is not. Von der Leyen is just one face of the biggest storyline of 2022: women acting as stalwarts for democracy.

American women suffered the greatest reversal of rights in the two decades of the list when the Supreme Court limited the right to an abortion.

In reaction, female voters energized U.S. mid-term elections. In Iran, thousands of women marched in the streets in protest against theocratic laws that treat them as second-class citizens.

Representing the protesters on this year's list is Jina "Masha" Amini, whose death in September sparked the unprecedented women-led revolution. The rest of the women are more traditional power players – 39 CEOs; 10 heads of state; and 11 billionaires worth a combined $115 billion.

The list was determined by four main metrics: money, media impact and spheres of influence. For political leaders, we weighed gross domestic products and populations; for corporate leaders, revenues and employee counts; and media mentions the reach of all. The result is a collection of women who are fighting the status quo.

"If you don't react to the first violation of your rights," says Roya Boroumand, an Iranian historian and human rights activist, "the second will come, and the third will come."

Thasunda Brown Duckett

In 2021, Thasunda Brown Duckett took over the heim of TIAA, a retirement and financial services company for academic, research, medical and governmental workers. The role makes her one of America's largest 500 companies, and one of the most powerful women in finance.

Taylor Swift

Taylor Swift became the first artist in history to claim the top ten spots on the Billboard Hot 100 song list. And in November, demand for tickets to her 2023 Eras Tour overwhelmed Ticketmaster, prompting members of Congress to question the company's hold on concert sales.

Falguni Nayar

Falguni Nayar worked as an investment banker for two decades, leading IPOs and helping other entrepreneurs achieve their dreams. In 2012, she decided to work for herself, investing $2 million of her own savings to launch beauty and retail company, Nykaa. She tbecame India's richest self-made woman.

Xiomara Castro

Xiomara Castro was sworn in as Honduras' president in January 2022, becoming the first woman to hold the position. Castro campaigned for the presidency on a platform that included protecting and expanding women's rights, but nearly one year into her tenure, feminist activists are losing hope that she will deliver on these promises.

The Power of Women Campaign

The Power of Women Campaign was created by a group of business leaders in the North-East who were sick and tired of young women in their region being constantly overlooked. Led by the late Professor Jane Turner OBE DL, together they came up with an action plan to improve the lives of young women in the Tees Valley and beyond.

Sadly, Professor Turner passed away in July 2021. However, Teesside University remains firmly committed to continuing her legacy and fully supports the campaign.

Deeply rooted attitudes fail young girls, stifling their aspirations and limiting their choices. What is more, the **World Economic Forum Global Gender Gap Report 2017 estimates it will be another 217** years before we achieve gender parity across the four areas of health, education, workforce and politics.

Professor Turner believed that today's young females have the power to change the world. The Power of Women Campaign works to help them realize their potential, by raising their aspirations and giving them the confidence to be who they are.

The **Power of Women Campaign** now has its own website, featuring a career assessment quiz as well as tools and resources to help young women and girls throughout their individual journeys. The website also houses some of the inspiring stories from role models across the North-East. By documenting their highs, lows and challenges, each role model exemplifies the grit and determination that resides in every woman in the North-East.

"The Women Power award is an annual award given by the Ministry of Women and Child Development of the Government of India to individual women or to instructions that work towards the cause of women empowerment."

"The strongest actions for a woman is to love herself, be herself and shine amongst those who never believed she could."

Introduction

The extent of empowerment of women in the national hierarchy is determined largely by the three faces – her economic, social and political identity and their weight-age. These factors are deeply intertwined and interlinked with many cross-cutting linkages which imply that if efforts in even one dimension remain absent or weak, outcomes and momentum generated by the other components cannot be sustained as they will not be able to weather any changes or upheavals. It is only when all the three factors are simultaneously addressed and made compatible with each other can the woman be truly empowered. Therefore, for holistic empowerment of the woman to happen – social, economic and political aspects impacting a woman's life must converge effectively.

Constitutional Provisions

Women as an independent group constitute 48% of the country's total population as per the 2001 Census. The importance of women as a important human resource was recognized by the Constitution of India which not only accorded equality to women but also empowered the State to adopt measures of positive discrimination in their favour. A number of Articles of the Constitution specially reiterate the commitment of the constitution towards the socio-economic development of women and upholding their political right and participation in decision-making.

Legislation and Laws for Women

The State enacted several women-specific and women-related legislations to protect women against social discrimination, violence and atrocities and also to prevent social evils like child marriage, dowry, practice of sati, etc. The recently notified **Prevention of Domestic Violence Act** is a landmark law in acting as a deterrent as well as providing legal recourse to the women who are victims of any form of domestic violence. Apart from these, there are a number of laws which may not be gender specific but still have ramifications on women.

National Politics for Women

The **National Policy for Empowerment of Women 2001** has its goal of bringing about advancement, development and empowerment of women in all spheres of life through creation of a more responsive judicial and legal system sensitive to women and mainstreaming a gender perspective in the development process. The strengthening and formation of relevant institutional mechanism and implementation of international obligations, commitments and co-operation at the international, regional and sub-regional level was another commitment.

The present government in their **National Common Minimum Programme** have laid down six basic principles of governance, one of which is to empower women politically, educationally, economically and legally.

International Commitments and Conventions and the MDG

India has ratified various international commitments and human rights conventions to secure equal rights of women. Key among them is the ratification of the conversation on **Elimination of all forms of Discrimination against Women** in 1993. India has ratified the convention with two declaratory statements and one reservation. Both the declarations relate to marriage. We have declared that the provisions on marriage and family relations in its Article would be to ensure in conformity with our policy of non-interference in the personal affairs of any community without its initiative and consent and that while agreeing to the principle of compulsory registration of marriages, failure to get the marriage registered at the same time will not invalidate the marriage. Eight Millennium Development Goals have been established in the at the General Assembly of the United Nations in the year 2000. These include promoting gender equality and empowerment of women and improving maternal health. Though only these two are explicitly gender specific, gender equality at the core of achievement of MDGs – form improving health and fighting disease, to reducing poverty and mitigating hunger, to expanding education and lowering child mortality, to increasing access to safe water, and to ensuring environmental sustainability.

Planning Process and Gender

The planning process has evolved over the years from purely "welfare" oriented approach where women were regarded as objects of charity to the development programmes and currently to their "empowerment." It was only from the Sixth Five Year Plan that women secured a special niche and space in the national plans and planning process primary with thrusts on health, education and employment of women. A paradigm shift occurred in the Eighth Plan where "empowerment" of women was recognized and accepted as a distinct strategy.

A further impetus for sector contribution to women's programme was received with the introduction of the concept of Women's Component Plan in the Ninth Plan whereby identified ministries were required to indicate the flow of funds to the women's programs and schemes. However, the Ninth Plan refrained from making any commitment for achieving any specific goal or targets were set for a few key indicators of human development.

The targets include, among other things, reduction in gender gaps in literacy and wage rates and reduction in MMR.

The Tenth Five Year Plan called for the three-pronged strategy of social empowerment, economic empowerment and providing gender justice to create an enabling environment of positive economic and social policies for women and eliminating all forms of discrimination against them and thus advance gender equality goals.

Status of Women – A Situational Analysis

Though the Constitutional commitments of the nation to women was translated through the planning process, legislation, policies and programs over the last six decades, yet as the eleventh plan approaches, a situational analysis of social and economic status of women reflect less than satisfactory achievements in almost all important human development indicators. The maternal mortality rate is estimated at 407 per 100,000 live births in India.

It is in these sectors that women predominately eke out a sustenance livelihood. The lack of employment, skill training, or credit facilities for women, who seek it, is another factor that keeps them in poverty.

Traditional patriarchal systems play their part in keeping women at a lower rung in the social and economic hierarchy by denying them basic rights to land, assets, etc and also placing a low value on their existence. The high prevalence of female foeticide and child marriage is a fall out of these factors.

The weak social infrastructure such as the lack of adequate schools or health centres, drinking water, sanitation and hygiene facilities inhibits a very large section of women from accessing these facilities. This is a major reason why women continue to face problems as poor literacy rates, or health issues. It is also one of the reasons for the high incidence of MMR and IMR.

The changing socio-economic scenario and the phasing out of the joint family system along with poor community based protection systems are some of the reasons why women are becoming insensitive of the various functionaries and fail to check the growing violence against women. At the same time, the extremely poor levels of awareness amongst women themselves on their rights also perpetuate violence against them. The lack of adequate rehabilitation and reintegration facilities is another crucial factor that finds victimized women further victimized or ostracized by the community. The media too does not reflect gender issues with sympathy and sensitivity; instead there is a tendency to glorify patriarchal traditions or to depict women.

Gender Concerns and Eleventh Plan – Path Ahead

Though for the first time, a separate section on 'Gender Equity' was included in the Draft Approach Paper to the 11th Five Year Plan, the paper has not been given enough focus on women's empowerment issues in the country. The strategy for women is confined to these areas – violence against women, economic empowerment of women has to be visualized as a holistic integrated approach and not in a piece meal manner or as water tight compartments. More often than not, the lines dividing social, economic or political areas are highly diffused and blurred with criss- crossing intersections.

Over the years efforts have been made to socially, economically and politically empower women but as a result of the lack of synergy or coordination between these activities, the outcomes could never be completely satisfactory. For example, the increasing induction of women representatives into the PRIs should have meant automatic improvement in the lives of rural women, but if it has not happened, it is because the elected women were not educated or literate or even made aware of their rights. Also, there are many groups of women who on account of tradition, culture, ethnic, social or religious background are more vulnerable as compared to the women in the mainstream sector. These groups need to be specially focused on in the Eleventh Plan.

It is imperative that an integrated policy and strategy be formulated that address economic, social, and political empowerment simultaneously and holistically along with the requisite programmes and schemes. Once such a comprehensive policy and programs flowing from it are put in place, it will be possible to enable an all round development of women, which will usher in true empowerment. This is the philosophy of empowerment which will be the plank on which the Eleventh Plan approach to women will be based.

Keeping in view the philosophy of empowerment it is essential that the Eleventh Plan should indicate clearly the direction that the planning process intends to take for women in the ensuing five years and delineate the thrust areas. An underlying thread that will form the essence of empowerment philosophy is 'gender equality and equality' and 'elimination of gender discrimination' – essential ingredients that must be inherent in the thrust areas and also be incorporated as an integral part not only in all programs and scheme for women, but also in the delivery mechanism and outreach services to the beneficiary.

Gender equality, is a constituent of development as well as an instrument of development. No country can be deemed developed if half the population is severely disadvantaged in terms of basic needs, livelihood options, access to knowledge, and political voice. It is an instrument of development because without gender equality other goals of development will also be difficult to achieve, namely the goals of poverty alleviation, economic growth, environmental sustainability, etc. A natural corollary of ensuring gender equality is the elimination of gender discrimination. Inequalities between girls and boys in access to schooling or adequate health care prove a very serious disadvantage to women and girls and limit their capacity to participate in the benefits of development.

Important Thrust Areas for the Eleventh Plan

The crucial areas of concern to a large extent, suggest the thrust areas that are required to be kept in view in the Eleventh Plan. While priority will continue to be laid on health, nutrition, education, income-generating activities, relief and rehabilitation for women in distress, there are certain key thrust areas which need to be addressed with a sharper focus. These are given below:

Nutrition and gender

It is acknowledged that the underlying reasons for poor health of women as well as high rates of MMR and IMR are the persisting problems of malnutrition and anemia. The Eleventh Plan will need to lay adequate stress on addressing both these problems with provision of adequate supplementary nutrition and micro-nutrient supplements.

Health and gender

The health issues of a woman if observed through a life cycle approach shows that various health problems persist right from the time she is conceived till her old age. The high rate of MMR needs to be addressed through improving the rate of institutional deliveries, training of midwife, ensuring that ANM and the primary health centres are operational. Adequate information on pre- natal care and post-natal care must be taken up on a priority basis.

Globalization and Women

With the growing globalization and liberalization of the economy as well as increased privatization of services, women as a whole have been left behind and not been able to partake of the fruits of success. The mainstreaming of women into the new and emerging areas of growth is imperative. This will require training and skill upgradation in emerging trades, encouraging more women to take up vocational training and employment in the boom sectors. This will also require women to migrate to cities and metros for work. Provision of safe housing and other gender friendly facilities at work will need to be provided.

Another facet of globalization is related to the fact that many persons especially women will be severely affected with the advent of setting up of industrial parks, national highways, SEZ ,etc. as huge tracts of farm land are likely to be acquired for this purpose. This would require massive resettlement of the displaced persons and their families. It is, therefore, essential that a viable resettlement policy and strategy is formulated and put in place immediately which clearly reflects the needs of women impacted by globalization.

Women in agriculture

With the growing feminization of agriculture, there is a need to develop specific strategies for women in agriculture. Apart from conferring land rights, it is also essential that MWCD work in close cooperation with agriculture to develop their skills and strengthen their capacities as well as access to cheap finance and other inputs. It is also important to strengthen organic farming which is very convenient and familiar to woman.

Institutional mechanism

Institutional mechanism for the advancement of women include institutions of different types – government, non-government, central and state government, local government, which support the cause of women's advancement. Institutional mechanisms for integrating 'gender perspectives in policy and planning include such innovative features as 'gender budgeting'. Though institutional mechanism exist both at the central and state levels, they need to be strengthened. The **National Policy for Empowerment** provides for strengthening the existing mechanism through interventions as may be appropriate and will relate to, among others, provision of adequate resources, training and advocacy skills to effectively influence macro-policies, legislation, programmes, etc. to achieve the empowerment of women.

The policy also provides for setting up of National and State Councils headed respectively by the Prime Minister and the Chief Ministers to oversee the operational of the policy on a regular basis and review the progress made in implementing the policy twice a year. The **National Development Council** will also be informed of the progress of the programme undertaken under the policy from time to time for advice and comments. The Planning Commission also in its mid-term appraisal of the Tenth Plan has suggested in its **Way Forward** to undertake a high-powered inter-ministerial review of gender justice in order to bring the Tenth Plan back on track regarding its commitment to gender justice or to consider a Prime Minister's Mission on Women, Children and Development.

Role of MWCD

The history of the present **Ministry of Women and Child Development**, the nodal agency for welfare, development and empowerment of women is also the history of how women as a specific group were viewed by the Ministry of Social Welfare. In the year 1986 a separate department for women and children was constituted under the aegis of Ministry of Human Resources Development, primary keeping in mind that women were valuable human resources, and therefore deserved more focused attention.

This also implied a subtle shift from 'welfare' to 'development' approach for these sections. In January 2006, the Department was elevated to the status of a full-fledged independent Ministry, thus implicitly bringing woman's issues into the forefront with greater focus and a larger mandate. It also meant that the MWCD would enhance its commitment to women through a wider range of programmatic interventions and outlays, and advocate gender mainstreaming of other sectors.

Due to the wide-ranging facets and nuances of the nature of women empowerment the programmatic interventions perforce cannot be restricted to any one particular sector or ministry/department. The responsibility has to be shared between sectors and between Ministers/ Development with adequate scope for convergence linkages.

Thus the role of MWCD includes policy formulation, conception of innovative programmes and their implementation, coordination with other sectors and state governments, gender budgeting, training and capacity building, monitoring the status of women and their rights. This would require that appropriate institutional mechanisms are in place both in the MWCD, other ministries as well as the State governments so that implementation, networking, coordination and convergence is possible.

Schemes of the MWCD

The scheme programs of the MWCD can broadly be categorized into those that contribute to the economic empowerment of women, those that provide rescue and shelter to women in need of care and protection and those that provide gender justice and safeguard the rights of women.

The flagship scheme for women of MWCD for holistic economic empowerment is **swayamsiddha**. The schemes for economic empowerment also include the **Support for Training and Employment Program** which aims to raise the incomes of rural women by updating their skills in the traditional sectors such as dairy development, animal husbandry, sericulture, handloom and social forestry. The Ministry has also set up support towards economic empowerment. **Swadhar** and **Short Stay Homes** have been set up to provide shelter and care services for women in distress. The Ministry also implements laws and legislations for women including **Dowry Prohibition Act, Protection from Domestic Violence Act, ITPA**, etc. in the Eleventh Plan. It is proposed to expand the scope and content of these schemes so as to reach more women and empower them economically and socially.

Women and the Economy

Introduction

Sustained and rapid growth rates are the most effective route to poverty reduction. However, the main challenge is to ensure that growth is pro-poor and pro-women. India's economy, on average, has grown at a rate of more than 8 per cent during the last three financial years, making it one of the fastest growing economies in the world.

This has been accompanied by a benign rate of inflation. The BRICS report identifies India as the only economy that will be capable of maintaining growth rates above 5 per cent till the year 2050. India's share of global GDP, in purchasing power parity terms, at 5.9 per cent in 2005 is the fourth highest in the world. In terms of share in world exports, India accounts for 0.9 per cent, with the value of exports in US dollar terms placed at US $100 billion.

The poverty level, which was 36 per cent in 1993-94, had come down to about 22 per cent in 2004-05. However, statistical indicators, do not fully capture India's recent economic achievements.

For example: there has been an increased focus on infrastructure investments such as development of the **Golden Quadrilateral, Bharat Nirman, The National Urban Renewal Mission** aimed to provide further impetus to growth. In addition, major development initiatives have been launched – the historic **National Rural Employment Guarantee Act; the National Rural Health Mission**, the expanded Sarva Shikha Abhiyan and the **National Cooked Mid-day Meal Programme.**

The above initiatives are indicative of the growing awareness of the multi-dimensional nature of development. It is a well acknowledged fact that the thrust on social and human development is an important plank of the next generation of policy reforms. The efforts are being complemented by a steep jump in budgetary outlays for social sectors, along with dedicated initiatives for removing poverty and increasing employment. The main task that needs to be undertaken during the 11TH FYP is to ensure that women are at the centre-stage of all the activities – economic, social and political.

Economic Growth, Poverty and Gender Inequality

There exists a two-way link between economic growth and poverty, and gender inequality. On one level, poverty and the lack of growth exacerbated gender disparities. Inequalities between girls and boys in access to schooling or adequate health-care were more acute among poor people than among those with higher incomes.

And while poor people had less access to such productive resources as land and credit, poor women generally had the least access of all. Similarly, girls' and women's health and schooling were more vulnerable to economic downturns than those of boys and men.

On another level, gender inequalities undermined the prospects for poverty reduction in fundamental ways. While disparities in basic rights, access to schooling, credit and jobs, and the ability to participate in public life took their most direct toll on women and girls, evidence showed that gender inequality hindered economic growth.

The rationale for economically empowering women is compelling for both - for its own sake and for other spill-over benefits. Research indicates that economic participation of women – their presence in the workforce in quantitative terms – is important not only for lowering the disproportionate levels of poverty among women, but also as an important step towards raising household income and encouraging economic development in countries as a whole.

Amartya Sen makes a compelling case for the notion the societies need to see women less as passive recipients of help, and more as dynamic promoters of social transformation, a view strongly buttressed by a body of evidence suggesting that the education, employment and ownership rights of women have a powerful influence on their ability to control their environment and contribute to economic development.

However, participation alone is not enough, quality of women's work is critical. A key challenge is to overcome a situation where women may gain employment with relative ease, but where their employment is either concentrated in poorly paid or unskilled job "ghettos," characterized by the absence of upward mobility and opportunity.

For example, women are most often concentrated in "feminized" professions, such as nursing and teaching, office work, care of the elderly and disabled termed "horizontal occupational segregation" – where they tend to remain in lower job categories than men.

Typically, because these functions are carried out by women, they are the lowest paid, in addition to offering limited or no opportunity for advancement.

The term "feminization of poverty" is often used to illustrate the fact that a substantial percentage of poor are women and that the gap between women and men in poverty has not lessened, but may well have widened in the past decade.

Further, globalization has dramatically changed the conditions under which the work for gender equality must be carried out, especially in high growth countries like India.

While globalization has generated opportunities for local products and entrepreneurs to reach international markets, it has at times intensified existing inequalities and insecurities for many poor women who already represent two-thirds of the world's poorest people.

Since the gains of globalization are often concentrated in the hands of those with higher education – those who own resources and have access to capital – poor women are usually less able to seize the longer term opportunities offered.

In the last two decades, this disadvantage has been exacerbated as in most of the countries, policies reflect a commitment to global norms of markets and social policy is increasingly determined by market dynamics. Market friendly policies generate high growth rates that fail to translate into improved standards of health, education and human security.

Feminist scholars have highlighted the gendered impact of such policies, many of which increase women's job vulnerability, unpaid work burden, while reducing state level resources that might be used to provide a social safety net.

Owing to dissent voiced by feminist scholars on the widespread assumption that gender inequality as a challenge can be overcome with effective and sustained advocacy as it is more about mindsets and less about policies, especially economic policies, there have been some attempts to integrate economic and social policies but gender concerns have not been accorded requisite attention. These disadvantages have led to a situation where gains in women's economic opportunities lag behind those in women's capabilities.

This is inefficient, since increased women's labour force participation and earnings are associated with reduced poverty and faster growth, women will benefit from economic empowerment but so too will men, children and society as a whole.

Women's lack of economic empowerment or other negative impacts including less favourable education and health outcomes for children is extremely important to ensure that women are economically empowered. There are various factors that contribute to the economic empowerment of women. These factors operate at various levels.

In the current scenario, one can identify the following characteristics of women's work in India:

1.   **Volatility of empowerment** – particularly export-oriented employment. In less than one generation, there had been massive shifts of women's labour into the paid workforce and then the subsequent ejection of older women and even younger counterparts into more fragile and insecure forms of employment. Women's livelihoods in rural areas had been affected by the agrarian crisis in most developing countries.

2.   **Changes in the nature of women's work** – including an increase in informal work, characterized by gender reliance on casual contracts and an increase in service work. There had been a substantial increase in self-employee low-end service work, especially in domestic and retail trade.

3.   **Increase in unpaid work** – the impact of the decline in the public provision of many basic goods and services had meant a substantial increase in unpaid work.

4.   **Crisis of livelihoods in agriculture prices** - Agriculture constituted the main employment of women in the developing world and the basic source of income for most of the world's poor.

5.   **Massive increase in women's migration for work** – what was new historically was the fact that women were moving alone. Cross-border migration had become a huge issue. While it had become a source of macroeconomic stability, it was also a source of exploitation. Internal migration had also increased. Migrant workers had few rights, and government rarely thought about ensuring their protection.

Enabling Strategies for Economic Empowerment of Women

Sound macro-economic policies – Gender inequalities manifest as women and men have different access to resources, roles and responsibilities, both in the market and at the household. These inequalities exist at the mezzo and micro levels with macro implications indicating clear two-way linkages. In the Indian context, fiscal policies are being increasingly examined through gender sensitive – budgeting exercises, although the focus still remains on expenditures in soft sectors, with several aspects like taxation, trade, capital flows, etc. remaining largely an unstudied domain. Macro-economic policies are formulated and implemented in areas such as trade, fiscal management, debt financing, social welfare and other sectors without a comprehensive assessment of their potential gender impacts. All these issues would be particularly important if the analysis of the sources of growth were to suggest that influencing the distribution of income and assets by gender might have a beneficial effect. Some policies, particularly those promoting health and education or promoting greater women's property rights and control over assets or access to credit, technology and transport are likely to be win-win policies in terms of higher growth, greater equality and reduced susceptibility of women to economic shock.

Recommendations

1.   Increasing the mainstream financial services available to women.

2.   Developing or adapting legal frameworks that eliminate the gender biases of financial institutions.

3.   Increasing inclusion of poor women and other vulnerable groups to give them a voice in economic bodies and financial structures.

4.   Supporting the incorporation of gender perspective into budget processes.

5.   Undertaking and disseminating gender perspectives into budget processes.

6.   Developing policy frameworks that allow women to move away from the ghetto of micro- finance to mainstream economic policy and structure.

7.   The Eleventh Plan should address the unpaid work of women in an explicit manner through a well-designed strategy that will inform all planning and programming for women.

8.   The Eleventh Five Year Plan should emphasize the need for collection of comprehensive data on women's paid and unpaid work, women's asset ownership. Banking policies had to include targeted credit.

9.   Micro-credit was not a panacea. It was necessary to reinstate the role of public institutional credit.

10.   Measures were also needed to reduce employment volatility and to increase public provision of basic services and goods, especially nutrition.

It was crucial that the crisis in agriculture be addressed, including the issue of trade protection and import regulation.

11.   Problem with gender budgeting was the obsession of how much was directed towards women. That did not say much about how fiscal policies were affecting women. The focus needed to be made broader.

Gender Equality in Inheritance Laws

The **Hindu Inheritance Law** has recently been reformed in a major way through the **Hindu Succession Amendment Act 2005**. This has brought woman on par with men in relation to agricultural land. However, the inheritance law governing Muslim women needs amendment for agricultural land and laws for tribal women need codification and formalizations in keeping with the principle of gender equality.

This has to be supplemented by proving legal literacy and legal support services for women.

Recording of women's shares

The NSS, agricultural census and the cost of cultivation surveys should collect gender disaggregated data on land ownership and use and origin of the property. Initially, this could be done as a special module on a pilot basis and later extended to the full surveys design. Agricultural universities that undertake surveys should also be asked to collect gender disaggregated information on land and other assets. A directive should be issued to all levels of government functionaries involved with keeping land records or computerizing and updating records that women's inheritance shares in land as widows, daughters, etc are fully and proactively recorded. The recording should be in women's own names, rather than joined with other relatives.

For improving women's access to public land

-       In case of displacement, a rehabilitation policy should ensure agriculture land of land policy, employment for agricultural workers who have been displaced, transfer of all rehabilitation and government grant of land to households having joint titles and resident communities affected by displacement who have a stake in the newly created assets in the region.

-       There needs to be comprehensive directive across the country that in all government land transfers, women's claims are directly recognized, be they transfers for poverty alleviation, income-generation, resettlement, etc.

- Where new to the comprehensive directive across the country that in all government land transfers, women's claims are directly recognized, be they transfers for poverty alleviation, income-generation, resettlement etc.

- In contrast, individual titles, half the land allocated to the family should be registered in the wife's name and half in the husband's name rather than jointly in both names. This will give women control over their shares and greater bargaining power. However, where possible a group approach should be followed, as is already being done under some government and NGO programmes. A group approach to land use need not be limited to crops. It could be extended to other activities such as fish production.

- Distribution of surplus land under all land distribution programmes viz, land ceiling act, custodial land, bhoom-dan land, etc should exclusively be distributed to rural landless women workers.

- Fifty per cent of the land pattas given to forest communities should go to women, under any land enactment, including those under the proposed **Scheduled Tribes Bill, 2005**. Rather than giving joint pattas, however, women and men should be given individual pattas. Also, any new land so distributed should be in terms of group rights.

For improving women's access to land via the market

- Apart from direct land transfer, the government should assist groups of women to collectively acquire cultivable land from the market, either on lease or via purchase. Special schemes for subsidized credit are needed for this. Mechanism can be devised to utilize the DWCRA or IRDP funds.

- Groups of poor women could be given land on medium or long-term leases, again for group farming or group fish production. Enabling women to undertake group leasing will fit in too with ongoing discussions on tenancy reform.

- The formation of such groups should not be limited to SHGs, since many SHGs are not composed of the poorest. Local NGOs could also be consulted and inducted into this for forming groups of poor women.

- It should be ensured that women get access to new options for land uses and must also ensure that these are not labour displacing and do not affect security negatively.

Strengthening women's agricultural capacities

The **Ministry of Agriculture** is now moving from a 'women only' approach to programming to the gender mainstreaming approach spread across the entire establishment.

Earmarking of benefits to women or of participation by women, though a basic tool, confines itself to the quantified dimension.

Other indicators of good program outcomes need to be identified so that an overall conclusion can be reached that the program and the funds invested, are making the women participants better off. Right now there are no such qualitative or measurement tools. Successful achievement of physical and financial target need not lead to empowerment or rise in status.

Better coordination and collaboration between the various intra-ministry formations is vital. A broader and more inter-disciplinary approach by all concerned can achieve better outreach to the poorer women working in the sector.

Public investment in agriculture should be 10% of GDP with a stipulation that 50% of the new investment be made in rural activities directly benefiting women.

Recommendations for strengthening women's agricultural capacities

o   Agricultural extension services and other infrastructural support for women farmers should be made available to women farmers.

o   Policies should be designed to ensure women's control over complementary resources including irrigation, credit, water, forest, fuel, fodder, information and training.

o   Design women friendly technologies. Technologies must be used that are safe for workers i.e. reduced use of pesticides, ensure that occupational safety and health measures are in place.

o   Training programs covering areas such as land surveying, resource mapping, resource management, use of technology, marketing, financial management cooperative management and organic farming should be made available to women.

o   Where possible women farmers should be given financial support to create assets either as individuals or as a group, including investing in small irrigation systems, etc.

o   Measures should be taken to remove middlemen in the sale of non-timber forest products and women's cooperatives for directly marketing these products should be formed.

o   Resource pooling and group investments in capital equipment; cooperative marketing.

Ensuring women's effective presence in village decision-making bodies

o   Women are major stakeholders in the protection of the environment, especially forests, it is critical that rural women are centrally involved in the institutions set-up for forest management across the country. All joint **Forest Management Groups** across the states should allow all village adults to become members of the groups. Also, these groups should have at least one-third and if possible, 50% women in their executive committees. Within each JFM executive committee, there should be a subcommittee composed only of women who can put forward women's collective concerns before the Executive Committee and General Body. Having one or two token women does not give women a say in the decisions. Where there are well functioning non JFM community forestry institutions, such as **van panchayats** in Uttaranchal, they should be strengthened rather than replaced by JFM, and made more gender balanced.

o   Gender sensitizing through the media, educational institutions, etc, for changing social norms and social perceptions.

Strengthen existing institutions

o   The National Gender Resources Centre should be strengthened to enable it to meet its gender commitments from a sounder technical and professional base. A better interface with the National Centre for Research on Women in Agriculture would contribute to this. Joint activities can be planned as part of the National Action Plan for Women.

Devise incentive mechanism

o   Increase subsidies to poor farmers and non-farm livelihoods providing incentives such as provision of higher subsidies for land development, irrigation, credit and rebate on transfer fee, house tax, sales tax and stamp duties on women-owned land, housing and rural industries.

Evolve a social security policy for farmers

o   Such a policy would aim to decrease the negative impact of globalization on agriculture and allied activities on women

o   Corrective measures aiming to mitigate farmer suicide like:

a)   waiving pending loans and debt of small and marginal farmers

b)   conducting a census of farmers who have committed suicide and paying liberal compensation to the victims' families and

c)   designing compensation package for women and children in impacted families.

Women Workers in the Unorganized Sector

The unorganized sector is large in India, accounting for 370 million workers in 1999-2000, constituting 93% of the total workforce and 83% of the non-agricultural work force.

Women account for 32% of the workforce in the informal economy, including agriculture and 20% of the non-agricultural workforce. 118 million women workers in India, the informal sector in the non-agriculture segment alone engaged 27 million women workers in India.

Women informal workers are concentrated mainly in agriculture – so much so that three-quarters of all employed women are in informal employment in agriculture. 90% of those employed in manufacturing and construction are also unorganized sector workers. Within manufacturing, they predominate in certain industries such as garments, textiles, food and electronics. The seasonality of work in this sector and the lack of other avenues of work make them vulnerable to a range of exploitative practices. They remain the most vulnerable and the poorest. And yet they are economically active and contributing to the national economy.

Home-based work

A large number of women work as home-based workers. About 23% of the non-agricultural workers were home-based or working in their own dwellings. Home-based workers were an overwhelming 57% of the workforce among women.

Home-based worker refers to the general category of workers who carry out remunerative work within their homes or in the surrounding grounds. Women turnout to become a home-based worker for a number of reasons.

Lack of necessary qualifications and formal training, absence of childcare support, social & cultural constraints and absence of alternatives are some of the reasons. Families need cash incomes for their survival. Loss in format employment and reduced returns from agriculture often result in men migrating to urban centres, leaving behind women and children. With home-based work being the only alternative available to poorest communities, it is not confined only to women but also involves children, especially girls. There are positive aspects to home-based work also. It gives women the opportunity to combine domestic chores, flexible and sometimes better working conditions. While designing strategies to meet the challenges, it is important to retain the positive aspects of home-based work.

Self-help groups and women's empowerment

The emergence and rapid multiplication of self-help groups based on micro-credit is a phenomenon that is gaining increasing importance in the development scenario. Today, there are seven million SHGs in the country. Nearly 90% of the groups are women only groups. SHGs have been viewed by the State as a strategy for both women's empowerment as well as poverty reduction. SHGs are a conduit for routing a wide range of government sponsored development messages and schemes. NGOs have increasingly been adopting SHGs as a strategy to bring women together, at a faster pace and larger scale than collective building processes adopted by them earlier. A number of powerful players, like MFIs, NGOs, corporations and donors, all of whom have a significant and growing interest in the SHG phenomenon with centres on poor women have entered the arena.

Credit is a right poor women must have access to. The experience of SHGs has shown that they have provided improved access to credit. Poor women are now perceived by the mainstream financial sector as credit worthy. Women have used savings and credit for needs such as those related to education and health, and in particular for crisis related needs. Participation in SHGs has meant opportunities related to mobility and a legitimate space in the public realm for leaders of SHGs. Notwithstanding all the positive achievements, the overall picture is uneven and raises some concerns related to gender justice and livelihoods that the 11th Five Year process needs to address. These concerns draw upon the understanding of equity and gender justice of concerned practitioners who have implemented SHG programmes as well as several research studies.

Women and the Law

The Constitution of India recognizes equal rights of women, the state to take special measures for women and children to realize the guarantee of equality. Despite different gender specific laws in place, women's status in society continues to be devalued. Gender-based violence and discrimination faced by women are manifestations of the devalued status of women. In order to find an enduring solution to gender-based violence, laws impacting on a woman's equality rights have to be assessed and strictly implemented. Laws prohibiting gender discrimination based in the home and in the public sphere have to be evolved and implemented. As this process will take place in the years to come, the aspect of gender year plan is on issues of gender-based violence. Simultaneous efforts to improve women's status through the use of laws will also be undertaken.

Prevalence of gender-based violence

Violence against women includes any act of gender-based violence that results in, or is likely to result in, physical, or psychological harm or suffering to women, including threats of such acts, coercion or arbitrary deprivation of liberty, whether occurring in public or private life. Violence against women manifests itself in many ways and is one of the most pervasive forms of human rights abuse in the world today. While all women may experience violence, it intersects with other social and identity-based constructs like caste, religion, ethnicity, disability and to make specific groups vulnerable to different and particular forms of violence. Thus, the nature of the violence and how it manifests itself may differ because of social location.

To effectively deal with the problem of violence against women efforts are being made to strengthen the existing legislation through review and amendments and develop institutional mechanisms. The support services, in place, to victims of violence are short stay homes, swadhar. help lines for women in distress, legal literacy and legal awareness camps, earmarking of one fast track court in a district, to deal exclusively with cases of violence against women, constitution of the National Commission for Women and state commissions, increased recruitment of women police officers, establishment of women police cells in police stations and exclusive women police stations and establishment. In addition to these, efforts are being made to sensitize judiciary, police and civil administration.

In India, women are entering the labour workforce in unprecedented numbers. In light of this development, there is, more than ever before, a pressing need for the rights of women to be respected, protected and fulfilled, particularly in the workplace. Further with greater representation of women in the unorganized sector there is a need for institutions and a policy to be set up to empower women.

Socio-Economic and Cultural Interventions for Vulnerable Groups

The first two categories comprising infants, children and young girls represent roughly half of the country's female population. Within these two categories, there are especially defenceless sub- groups, such as the girl children of tender years, when discrimination in matters such as food intake, health and medical care, schooling, recreational facilities, etc. is entrenched both within families as well as communities as well as larger social formations. Another group consists of girls stepping from childhood to adolescence, facing a new grown-up world, with very little preparation of learning, knowledge or skills, or of how to come to terms with their own patriarchal environment.

While age is an important maker in categorizing women, there is also the necessity of looking at other criteria such as those based on certain socio-economic differentials. Besides looking into women, on the whole, as a discriminated lot, it is important to reflect on the Eleventh Plan repeatedly emphasizing the need to restructure growth as a board and inclusive process.

It frankly admits that even the achievement of reaching broad-based and inclusive growth will not suffice to reach "certain marginalized groups" and that the Eleven Plan must pay special attention to the needs of these groups.

Whilst developing the theme of deprivation and scarce access to social services, it is accepted that the most deprived groups among the poor are rural women, urban slum women, dalits, adivasis, backward classes and other categories as detailed in the chapter on introduction of this Report.

In fact, viewing women as a distinctly separate group misses out the intersections between gender and other variables of social and economic status.

These intersections reinforce vulnerability of more than one type and result in double and triple discrimination amongst women belonging to these groups. It is necessary not only to unravel these threads and trace several distinctive roots of inequality and discrimination, but also to conceive of multilayered responses in planning and programming in order to bridge the divide using the theme of 'inclusive growth'.

"While gender is undoubtedly an independent source of vulnerability, what is of particular concern is the way class, social and gender relationships reinforce one another in order to increase the insecurity and vulnerability of poor, low caste women" Srivastava.

The proposition is that there is a certain predisposition to being deprived of human development opportunities, even where these opportunities, state provided or otherwise, exist for the men and women of these communities. What is less recognized is a woman exacerbates the conditions of being poor, illiterate, landless, assetless and suffering from poor health morbidity or malnutrition.

Women from Scheduled Castes and Scheduled Tribes

The stark disparities in access to human development amongst girls in the country are well brought out by the data above. It brings out the crucial need to not only see social, economic and gender disparities within the same frame, but also provide responses that integrate all these concerns.

There are some welcome initiatives emerging from the **Ministry of Human Resource Development**. Special attention is being paid to districts identified as low female literacy districts for scheduled castes and scheduled tribes. The proposal is to launch national programs of elementary education in these areas.

Another welcome initiative by the Ministry is to cross match indicators of educational backwardness such as minority concentrations, tribal and draw up lists of such districts for introducing program interventions.

Looking at subordinate status of women and girls and as a systemic feature at all levels of society would seem to be only belabouring the point.

But sector development planning often fails to catch the extent of gender discrimination across social grouping in situations of double and triple-pronged exclusion. Interventions for girls cannot and or should not stop at narrowing the gender gap, but also bridge the divides of social, caste and religious groupings. Support to human development through affirmative action has to straddle both gender and social divides.

It is here that the provisions of both the constitution are to be synergized.

Instruments of gender planning such as national and state action plans for women, perspective plans for women, gender budgets, gender audit, etc. should pay sufficient attention to the problem of reaching women of particular groups, communities and categories to help them catch up.

Conversely, affirmative programs and other similar groups being administered by the concerned Ministries should pay attention to gender as well as caste tribe which is not the case now.

A scan of Government documents reveals gender gaps in affirmative action programs meant for such disadvantaged groups. But the provisions do not respond to the capacity building needs of women and girls of these groups, who are facing double deprivation of caste and gender. A few illustrative examples are given below.

There is no special consideration for "being female" in these grants, through the poor educational status of scheduled caste and scheduled tribe girls.

Other such gender muted instances of affirmative action include reservation of seats for candidates in IIT's, IIM's, Regional Engineering colleges, Central Universities, Kendriya Vidyalayas, and Navodaya Vidyalayas, etc. These are amongst the most prestigious educational and professional institutions run under the aegis of the central government throughout the country.

The issue is whether multiple disadvantages can be captured and responded along a single axis. Data shows that whether it is women and girls of minority communities or socially disadvantaged groups or those suffering from disability or the aged, for all of them, several axes of disadvantage operate simultaneously. Absence of social gender focus in affirmative action in favour of socially marginalized groups often means accepting the fall back position of making choice on the basis of merit, a criterion that has negated the vision of social and gender empowerment in the larger context.

The effects of gender on schooling, as brought out in a survey of Bihar and UP show girls from poor low caste households as having the least access to education.

Since both the states are educationally backward, the overall enrolment rates are poor and so are the female enrolment rates, with wide gender disparities. Among each social group and within each quintile, lesser numbers of girls are enrolled, indicating the importance of gender as a factor determining access to education. In the lowest quintile, nearly two-thirds of girls are out of school, . But it is the girls from the poor, low caste households who have the least access to education.

The researchers observed, "the largest educational differential is between poor low caste girls and rich upper caste males in these areas, showing how social, economic and cultural relations reinforce each other to the determinent of this group of girls." While this provides a gender comparison, the data also sow the steep differential between the enrolment rates of the poorer low caste.

Disaster-affected women

Experiences have shown that disaster, however 'natural', is profoundly discriminatory. Wherever they hit, pre-existing structures and social conditions determine that some members of the community will pay a higher price. Among the differences that determine how people are affected by such disasters is that of gender.

Women's lower status in general results in various kinds of exclusions and vulnerabilities in a disaster setting. Low mobility and lower access to information implies that women are often the last to receive relief resources. Women are disproportionately represented within the informal and agricultural sectors, which are the most adversely affected by disasters. This adversely affects their claim to relief and rehabilitation. Thus, women experience high rates of unemployment, even further decreasing their bargaining power within households and communities. Unlike men, they are the primary household caretakers and thus are not able to migrate for work. All these factors involving structural biases and gender discrimination results in the compensation amounts awarded being directed invariably at men.

Furthermore, domestic violence against women sharply increases after disasters and women face additional kinds of physical violence in relief camps. In the face of disasters where men die, are injured or migrate, women are left to lead households and communities, with few marketable skills and opportunities and even more vulnerability to violence and extortion, women take on the responsibility for both caring for families and meeting livelihoods while having the least access to information, resources and opportunities.

Disasters create the potential to engage in long-term rights and equity-based development through critical and practical strategies for gender empowerment. Successfully incorporating women within disaster management and mitigation is one way to increase women's social, political and economic status in general, and to minimize the currently disproportionate impact of disasters on women. Strategies include strengthening the marketable skills of women, promoting livelihood options, enhancing women's leadership in micro-planning relief and disaster mitigation and increasing their role in local governance.

Practically, women have immense knowledge of their local environments and information about how to mitigate risks that lead to disasters. This knowledge can be transformed into actionable expertise by involving women within disaster management.

Furthermore, women are the most effective in mobilizing communities, networks and institutions to pool resources, respond to disaster and create safety mechanisms.

Women in the North-East

The situation in the North East is rooted in lack of income and employment. The North East policy of the GOI could be a valuable device to open opportunities. Of special attention are issues related to introducing new avenues for non-farming activities of women – food processing, bottling, canning and packaging. Attention needs to be paid to creating job oriented skills for manufacture of indigenous products, popularizing indigenous cuisine in the potential tourist areas and highways, skills in hotel management, creating travel guides to depict North East histories, cultures and traditional assets, etc.

Women are the most vulnerable section of society in border trade centres and areas, which are adjacent to international borders and normally a 'no man's land' controlled by anti-social elements and organizations that are inimical to the interests of the country. Under these circumstances, women, who are the major component in border trades, especially in agriculture and allied activities, are under severe threat. Matters are compounded by problems of infrastructures and facilities, which are either most rudimentary or simply do not exist. Access to health, education, drinking water and sanitation, etc, is almost impossible, which adversely affects health.

Border trade centres besides being beds of smuggling, particularly of narcotics, also are centres of trafficking of women and children. Women are rendered vulnerable to all kinds of diseases, especially. Women are also used or forced into smuggling of narcotics, which makes them further vulnerable to law enforcing agencies that are not sensitized to dealing with women law breaker. The circle gets more vicious for women in these areas, many of whom are either illiterate or have received only rudimentary education and cannot be expected to be aware of their fundamental, human, legal and other rights. Problem of communication, organized marketing and non-implementation of labour laws also adversely affect women's economic power, which in turn reinforces them to play subservient roles and their empowerment continues to remain illusionary and elusive.

It is, therefore, suggested that some mechanism is set-up in border trade centres to enforce the law of the land, and also to implement and monitor all fundamental, human, legal and other rights to ensure that no citizen of this country is denied and deprived of them.

Enhancing the utilization of the region's local and rich natural resources with appropriate technology for producing and marketing herbal products and processed food fruits is another avenue to meet with the challenge posed by anti-social elements. Cold storages can be located in appropriate areas of the region, to sustain perishable items before they are transported to larger markets.

Recommendations

1.   The legal framework on disability makes no provisions for women with disabilities. The **PWD Act** is gender neutral. It does not address the specific concerns of women with disabilities in the areas of health, education and employment. A gender-based analysis of existing legislation on disability would go a long way in highlighting both the obstacles faced by women with disabilities and their possible remedies.

2.   Anecdotal reportage by doctors reveals that they see most disabled females only as children when parents come for treatment for their disability. Rarely are they seen in obstetric and gynaecological settings as adults. Reproductive health of women with disabilities in another grey area which does not even find a mention in the RCH programmes.

3.   Women with disabilities are particularly vulnerable to violence and abuse. They may not have accurate knowledge about their bodies, abuse prevention and self-protection.

4.   Women with disabilities are quite often excluded from gender equity programmes. They should be included not only as beneficiaries but also as fieldworker and project facilitators, surveys designers and field investigators in projects with disability components. This will enhance their visibility in highly positive roles and challenge negative attitudes that reduce them to objects of pity and helplessness.

5.   Various levels of state administration and NGO sector dealing with welfare of women need to be oriented on the problems of women with disabilities. This would ensure that the diversity of women's experiences is part of the agenda of the women's movement and the structures within the state that focus on women and child development.

6.   There is a need for more sensitization workshops especially with women's groups and govt. departments like Ministry of Women and Child Development.

7.   There should also be a separate wing for women with disabilities in the Disability Commissioner's office. Women with disabilities should be represented on the central and state co-ordination and executive committees.

8.   Besides personnel dealing with women's welfare, health care staff should also be trained to respond to needs of women and girls with disabilities. Similarly, police and judiciary should also be trained to handle cases involving women with disabilities in a sensitive manner.

9.   Negative media representations of women with disabilities further reinforce negative public perception as women with defects. There is an urgent need to develop and propagate more realistic and positive images of women with disabilities as capable and productive persons in the mass media especially radio and television. Inclusive programming and highlighting the achievements of women with disabilities will go a long way in changing entrenched mindsets and creating positive role models for disabled girls. Such role models provide a subject with a face and success story worthy of emulation.

10.   There is a need to develop support services for families with a disabled member. As principal caregivers, mothers are particularly vulnerable to emotional stress. The situation is exacerbated for mothers who are particularly vulnerable to emotional stress. The situation is exacerbated for mothers of disabled daughters, who also suffer the taint of disability as those who did not only produce sons but instead gave birth

to a bigger burden for their families in the form of a daughter with a disability.

11. There is immense scope for gender mainstreaming within pedagogy. Whether it is courses in special education, rehabilitation or women's studies, the concerns of women with disabilities should feature as a special module if not as a separate course in itself. **Rehabilitation Council of India** can go a long way in promoting this process, since it is the agency responsible for standardising teaching and curricula in the disability sector in the country. So a two-pronged approach in training is the need of the hour, namely gender mainstreaming in curricula on disability and rehabilitation, and disability mainstreaming in curricula on gender and women's empowerment.

12. Allocation of funds to NGOs in the disability sector is also an area amenable to gender mainstreaming. Projects focusing on the welfare of women with disabilities should be promoted or a gender component built into any project that receives support.

13. Technology is also a path to empowerment. Government policies in the disability sector encourage development of innovative adaptive technologies. For instance, the scheme on science and technology projects in mission mode in the **Ministry of Social justice Empowerment** provides 100% research funding for such work. There is a need not only to make such technologies women-friendly but also to involve women with disabilities in their development.

14. The need of the hour is gender mainstreaming in curricula on disability and rehabilitation, and disability mainstreaming in curricula on disability and rehabilitation and disability mainstreaming in curricula on gender and women's empowerment.

Migrant Women

Internal short-term migration for work is now a widespread feature of rural India and reflects the continuing crisis of inadequate livelihood opportunities in rural areas. Increasingly, women are moving for work, not only with husbands or male members of families, but even on their own or in groups in search of work. Since the consequences of such migration are highly gendered, policies generating and more prolonged job opportunities for men and women particularly rural areas must be considered.

The estimation of migrants based on NSS 55th round for India is 245 million persons, that is 27 per cent of the population. More than half of total migrants were in the category of rural females. In general, females are far more migratory than males and the percentage of migrants to the total population was higher in urban areas than that in rural areas. The share of female migrants in both urban and rural female population reflects the high propensity to migrate around 42 per cent.

The migrant labourers generally work at whatever they can find, which is a combination of contract work of the Nirman departments or casual work in fields, or any other casual work they can get. The condition of migrant workers away from their homes is often pitiable. They get paid very less; they do not have access to clean water or sanitation. Often they do not have access to health care. They do not have access to public distribution system and have to buy their essentials at open market prices. Their children travel around with them and do not get an education.

Male out-migration, when the families are left behind, affects the work burden of the women in rural areas. Women have to put in extraordinary amount of time to eke out a living – working in the field – for wages or for subsistence, in addition to fetching fuel and fodder. The absence of men adds to material and psychological insecurity, leading to pressures and negotiations with a wider family. Women may have to cope with a number of problems which are exacerbated due to the uncertainly of the timing and magnitude of remittances on which the precarious household economy depends. This in turn, pushes women and children from poor labouring households to participate in the labour market under adverse conditions. The impact of male migration can be especially adverse for girls, who often have to bear additional domestic responsibilities and take care of younger siblings. The absence of male supervision further reduces their chances of acquiring education. Incidence of women headed households may also increase and it is to be noted that female-headed households are generally poorer than male-headed households.

The wages of the migrant husbands are either too infrequent or not enough for constant sustenance of the family left behind. Several micro studies have shown that it is the free and hard work of women in sustaining the domestic economy, which helps to keep a large number of men working in town and cities at extremely low wages.

Migrants suffer from a lack of access to health services both at home and in the work places, although they are known to be especially vulnerable

to health problems, and can serve as carriers of communicable diseases
. Mobility and migration of workers make them more vulnerable, as a
result of separation form spouse and release of social sanctions leading to
practices.

Additionally, explicit public policy with respect to migration should
cover issues affecting households of migrant workers, who are left without
adult caregivers. It should also cover issues to protection and basic needs
of migrant workers at their destination. Since women migrant workers
face much greater threats to security and possibilities of violence, special
measures should address this problem.

All the above points are only an illustrative list of the action areas for
women in vulnerable situations. There are many more such categories of
women, as seen from the list compiled in this chapter. As and when the
need arises specially designed projects will be formulated to address their
problems.

Social Empowerment

Women and girls in India face a crisis of growing and un-addressed health
needs. From the moment of conception to the end of life, the challenges to
the female are enormous, especially poor women who have limited access
to health care.

Education

Education is a key intervention in initiating and sustaining processes of
empowerment. Good quality education can help women and marginalized
communities improve their status, enable them to have greater access to
information and resources and to challenge various forms of discrimination.
Education helps strengthen democratic process as it allows for greater and
more equitable participation. Being educated or literate leads to greater
self-confidence and self-esteem, it enables engagement with development
processes and institutions of governance from a position of strength. Poor
women from socially disadvantaged communities are invariably not literate
and therefore, find themselves at a disadvantage participating in development
processes. They are unable to take full advantage when participating in
development processes. They are unable to take full advantage of progressive
measures like reservations in PRIs. Many of the negative fallouts of being
outside the education net for women are quite recognized, however the
articulation of the problem trends to remain at the level of rhetoric.

It is however, important to recognize that while being literate or educated is necessary for empowerment it does not automatically ensure it.

For that we need an education that is of good quality and promotes critical thinking. From the perspective of gender this means that education and literacy should enable women and girls to critically analyse their situations, raise questions about their subordination and help them make informed choices.

It is well known that the institution of schooling is an important site for socialization, that actually can reinforce rather than challenges patriarchy and gender discrimination. It is in this context that the content and pedagogy of education become critical considerations.

The focus of educational planning is on formal education but this is only one dimension of the educational provisioning. Especially when considering the needs of deprived women and when women's empowerment is our main aim, there is a need to think about well developed and structured educational interventions outside the formal system.

Capacity-building interventions are in essence educational and learning processes and must therefore be invested in well designed and conceived as a sustained, rather than adhoc process. Such interventions must necessarily be broad based and flexible and address a number of different needs, including literacy.

Sarva Shiksha Abhiyan

o   The XI plan through the SSA should pay attention to specific groups, context and locations and design programmes accordingly.

o   The groups should be reached through special projects within SSA.

o   Educational data should be gender disaggregated but should also be collected in terms of other social groupings.

o   Systematic mapping of social groups should be undertaken to sharpen planning and programme design processes.

o   In order to improve the educational status of Muslim girls and women and to bring them into the mainstream, policy measures and specific programmes backed by resource allocation needs to be put in place on an urgent basis.

o   A sub-plan on Muslim girls education should be constituted, which can act as a national task force, which should draw on could be set in place.

o   The number of formal schools in areas with a high Muslim population should be increased.

o   However, at the same time the community leaders should be sensitized to enable their girl children to attend schools and for retraining them in school system.

o   In order to arrest high drop-out rates after primary school attention SSA should be extended to the secondary school level. Attention should be paid to infrastructural issues like sanitation, etc. Incentive schemes can be thought of after a review of the existing schemes.

o   Programmes like the NPEGEL and KGVB which focus on girls should be continued and strengthened.

o   The policy of hiring female teachers should be continued. Strategies to increase the pool of female teachers from socially disadvantages groups and Muslims should be adopted.

Adult Literacy and Learning

o   Given the important role it plays in sustaining women's empowerment, women's collectives including self-help groups and its commitment to adult literacy and education should be rearticulated and backed by adequate resources.

o   The **National Literacy Mission** should be adequately resourced and revitalised. The CE programme should be revamped and innovative programmes designed with the participation of women's groups and other civil society organizations. As the literacy, rates of women from marginalised communities is far worse such programmes should address the specific needs of different groups.

o   The programme content should combine literacy with livelihoods and other survival issues and organization building. Lessons from the **Mahila Samakhya Programme** should be taken on board.

o   Equivalency programmes and certification system should be set in place for adult learners to enable them to take advantage of the various opportunities opening up. This can be done through the open learning mode and by expanding the mandate of NIOS.

o   A comprehensive capacity building programme which includes gender, legal literacy, livelihoods and literacy should be designed and a mechanism for its transaction put in place for women emerging in leadership position through SHGs.

Gnder Budgeting and Women Component Plan

The **National Common Minimum Program** lays down empowerment of women politically, educationally and legally as one of the six basic principles. To provide an impetus to this objective the Finance Minister in the budget speech for 2004-05 highlighted the perceived need for budget data to be presented in a manner that highlights the gender sensitiveness of the budgetary allocations. This was followed by a more emphatic commitment in the budget speech of 2005-06, wherein the budgetary allocations under 10, demand for grants estimated were highlighted in a separate statement as a part of the Gender Budgeting exercise. The 2006-07, Budget Speech revealed an estimated allocation for benefit of women under 24.

In spite of these commitments and focus on women's development and empowerment, the present status of women continues to be quite dismal in terms of important human development parameters like health, nutrition, literacy, educational attainments, skill levels, occupational status, etc. And there are a number of gender specific barriers, which prevent women for gaining access to their rightful share in the flow of public goods and services. Unless the felt needs of women are incorporated and mainstreamed in the planning and development process it is apprehended that the fruits of economic growth are likely to completely bypass a significant section of the country's population which does not augur well for the future growth of the economy. This calls for a focused priority in the Eleventh Plan for the strengthening, expansion and universe of gender budgeting in all its aspects.

Gender Budgeting

Gender Budgeting is defined as the application of gender mainstreaming in the budgetary process. It encompasses incorporating a gender perspective at all levels and stages of the budgetary process and paves the way for translating gender commitments to budgetary commitments and carrying out an assessment of the budget to establish its gender differential impact

In other words, gender budgeting looks at government budget from a gender perspective to assess how it addresses the needs of women not only in traditional areas like health, education, etc but also in so called 'gender neutral' sectors like transport, power, telecommunications, defence, etc. it does not seek to create a separate budget but seeks to put in place affirmative action for meeting women's specific needs, thus bringing into effect gender responsive budgeting.

The ultimate objective of gender budgeting is to transform and transcend traditional perceptions and mindsets toward women and awaken a gender sensitive consciousness which will not only enable women to come into the mainstream but also give them their due recognition as equal citizens of the country.

Budgeting for gender equity: A step forward in gender mainstreaming

The **Ministry of Women and Child Development** in 2004-05 adopted the mission statement of 'Budgeting for Gender Equity'. In 2005-06 the task was to carry forward this exercise of universalizing gender budgeting exercises in the centre and the states. Several initiatives have been undertaken by MWCD to operational gender budgeting. A strategic framework of activities to implement "Budgeting for Gender Equity" disseminated to all Departments identifies areas for gender mainstreaming including quantification of allocation of resources for women in union-state local budgets, gender audit of policies of governments, impact assessment of various schemes, analyzing programmes and strategies, institutionalizing generation and collection of gender disaggregated data, consultations and capacity building, etc. Further, guidelines for gender sensitive review of public expenditure and policy were farmed in the form of checklists both for beneficially oriented sectors development, labour, drinking water, textiles, agriculture, etc and for mainstream sectors that may appear "gender neutral" like defence, power, telecom, transport, etc. The Ministry has conducted several workshops and training programmes to disseminate the tools of gender budgeting and has advocated that a review may be undertaken with respect to.

1.   Gender-based profile o of public expenditure

2.   Beneficiary needs assessment

3.   Impact analysis

4.   Participative budgeting and

5.   Spatial mapping.

The MWCD has requested ministries to set up gender budgeting cells to undertake review of the public expenditure and policy, guide and undertake collection of gender disaggregated data, conduct gender-based impact analysis, beneficiary needs assessment and beneficiary incidence analysis.

As a result of these effort, 43 ministries/departments have set up gender budget cells as a nodal agency for all gender responsive budgeting initiatives.

Women's Component Plan

The women's component plan was the first major initiative taken by the government to address women related issues and requirements on a systematic basis involving the inputs from major ministries/ departments. The Women's Component Plan involved efforts to ensure that not less than 30 per cent of fund benefits were earmarked for women under the various schemes.

However, performance on the WCP has been disappointing and the mid-term appraisal of the Tenth Plan notes that while "the Department of Education has confirmed a flow of funds of the gross budgetary support to the WCP, the Ministry of Labour, which had reported flow of its budget during first three years of Tenth Plan." Several ministries and departments, which had earlier reported on the WCP in their sector budgets, have stopped doing so.

It also noted that there are some ministries and departments, which have the potential to go beyond 30 per cent of funds under WCP as well as devise and administer women related programmes.

These include Education, Health, Family Welfare, Environment and Forests, Rural Development, Agriculture, Labour, Urban Affairs, Drinking Water Supply, Tribal Affairs, Social Justice and Empowerment and possibly others. It also pointed out that the ministries and departments "that have defaulted in providing WCP allocations or whose WCP is less than 30 per cent of their budgets are advised to immediately take the necessary steps to make amends."

Taking the essence and intent of the mid-term appraisal of the Tenth Pan, WCP would need to be extended to all ministries and departments and not confined to the realm of some ministries and departments which have historically been perceived as "women related."

Simultaneously the implementation process of gender budgeting needs to be institutionalized and universalized in all the ministries and department at the centre and states.

WCP to continue as a bridging mechanism has to ensure that the momentum of flow of funds to women related programmes is sustained. WCP will require to be strengthened and to cover all sectors and schemes and all programmes both in the centre and the states.

Hitherto the emphasis of WCP has been on women related and women specific schemes. However, as women comprise nearly 50% of the population in the country, it is inevitable that all schemes and programs of the government, irrespective of the sector, will impinge on women in one way or another.

As such it is firmly believed that there is no sector program scheme that does not have gender implications. Hence, the strong recommendation of the sub groups is to extend the concept of WCP to all sectors in the centre and the states.

At least 30 per cent of the funds for all schemes is to be earmarked for women beneficiaries. For this purpose the ministries should identify women related schemes or engender existing schemes so that women can get the benefits under such schemes.

The essential earmarking of 30% funds for women under the WCP for all ministries at the centre and the states is at the very least a good exercise as it forces the policy makers to start thinking on the lines of gendered impact of policies. This commitment of resources is both vital and necessary.

Beneficiary incidence is an important part of WCP. It should be ensured that at least 30 per cent of the beneficiaries should be women.

PRIs should be intensively involved to ensure earmarking for women. As per the **Seventy Third Constitutional Amendment**, subjects have been transferred to the Panchayats. The schemes falling under these subjects could be looked into by the Panchayats to ensure implementation of WCP.

To ensure that funds actually reach the women, a non-lapsable pool of women's fund could be created in every state and also at the centre. If there is under utilisation of funds allocated for women specific programmes schemes under any Ministry, the balance amount of funds should be transferred to this pool.

Funds from this non-lapsable pool should be transferred to MWCD for utilizing the same in women related programmes.

At present, WCP treats women as one homogenous group but in reality, there are layers of discrimination even within women. Thus some women are more vulnerable than others. For example, a dalit woman will be doubly discriminated and a differently able dalit woman will be even more vulnerable. Thus WCP needs to factor in this intersectional framework while addressing issues of most vulnerable women, like dalit women and adivasi women.

Planning Commission should hold a quarterly meeting to review the progress of WCP. It should mandatorily obtain the information on WCP from ministries and states as a part of the Annual Plan exercise. The proposals submitted by the ministries and departments and the states should document the progress of the WCP during the current previous year and the steps proposed to be taken during the forthcoming year. Revised needs to be devised which should be simple and user- friendly in order to collect information on WCP.

Review of and effective implementation of all legislations and laws with a gender perspective to eliminate all forms of discrimination and violence against women

The laws and legalization are the framework that provide women her rights as equal citizens of the country. There are over 42 women-specific and related legislations.

Some women specific legislation include the **Immoral Traffic Act 1956, Maternity Benefit Act 1961, Dowry Prohibition Act 1961, Protection of women from Domestic violence Act 2005**, etc which seek to protect.

The women related legislations which have economic implications include the **Factories Act 1948, Minimum Wages Act 1948, Equal Remuneration Act, 1976**, etc many of which have provisions for providing economic justice and fair wages to women. There are other acts which are protection oriented such as **Pre-conception and Prenatal Diagnostic Technique Act 1994, Child Marriage Restraint Act and those with social implications like Family Courts Act 1984, Hindu Succession 1956, Indian Divorce Act 1969.**

Thus while there are a plethora of acts existing for the protection and socio-economic equality of women, it is only through tier effective implementation that women receive the intended benefits. However, gaps still remain and it is essential that specific laws are brought into effect which provides adequate safeguards and protection to women.

One such very important act is the compulsory registration of marriage act, which will protect the marital rights of the women and ensure her rightful share in the husband's property. A review of the legislation is also required to bring about conformity in the laws. In this context, it may be noted that necessary provisions of Indian Penal Code be brought in harmony with the provisions of the women relate acts so that there is no dichotomy between the different legislation.

Institutional Mechanism

Institutional Mechanism for the advancement of women includes institutions of different types which support the cause of women's advancement. The various institutional mechanisms that contribute to the achievement of women's empowerment and gender equality as laid down in the Eleventh Plan are listed below:

o   Government structures with a mandate for women such as ministries, departments, focal points, bureaus, cells, desks, coordination units and committees, inter agency committees, etc.

o   Government sponsored dedicated agencies for women, such as commissions, boards, committees, councils, corporations, women's resource centres, women's study centres, grass roots formations such as Mahila Mandals, self-help groups, etc.

o   The parliamentary committee on the empowerment of women.

o   Institutions of local government such as the three-tiered panchayats and urban local bodies which are to be delegated vast administrative, financial and legal powers across the development sectors, including social and women's development.

o   Mechanism and plans such as gender budgets, component plans for women, action plans for women, monitoring and assessing instruments such as HDR's, audit systems such as gender and social audit, appraisals and evaluations using tools such as gender analysis, participatory exercises, etc. To these can be added grassroots innovations capturing attention such as the Jan sunwais in the style of courts or other judicial bodies.o Women's bodies and groups working for the economic, social and political rights of women, all bearing the 'voluntary' and 'democratic' label, but with varying emphasis on different belief systems, ideologies and philosophies, etc. ranging from academia, research, education, feminism, to action research and advocacy.

o   Federations, trade unions, cooperatives, youth and other age base groups adhoc groups formed for short term objectives, watch dog bodies, local groups, etc.

The National Policy for Empowerment of Women had announced formation of National and State Council to oversee the operational of the policy on an ongoing basis. The National Council was to be headed by the prime minister, and the state council by the chief ministers.

They had to be broad in composition, with officials as well as central and state social welfare boards, National and State Commissions, NGOs, women's organizations, trade unions, academics, expert, social activists, etc.

These bodies were to meet twice a year and review the progress made in implementing the National Policy. Further, the National Development Council, the highest body in the government hierarchy, which has to officially approve all the five year plans, was also to be informed of the progress of the programmes undertaken under the policy from "time to time" and their advice sought.

Other commitments made in the policy on institutional mechanisms include setting up of state resource centres which would be linked with the women's study centres functioning in the country. At the district level, the existing institutions would be strengthened and at the grassroots women's groups would be helped to federate as registered societies at panchayats and municipal level. They would also be involved in the implementation of the policy.

The policy also announced the operational strategy for converting the policy into concrete programs on the ground. This was to be done trough the mechanism of the National and State Action Plans. These plans would be time bound and implemented in a participatory manner and also involve all the institutional machineries in the country.

The requirements of gender mainstreaming calls for close coordination between MWCD and other ministries and departments that are involved in the empowerment of women and gender equality.

The setting up of gender budgeting cells in more than 40 ministries and departments at the national level has the potential of taking the preparation and implementation of the plan of action forward.

Recommendations

o　　An apex body at the National level, as envisaged in the 2001 policy should be set up at the earliest, so that a comprehensive picture of the Action Plans can be prepared and reviewed.

o   Similarly, the policy commitment of reporting on progress of women's plans to the National Development Council from time to time should be implemented at the earliest.

o   Action plans for women's empowerment at national and state levels should be drawn up in consultation with civil society including women's groups, lawyers, activists, women's studies centres, etc.

o   While action plans should receive inputs from all sector agencies the format of the plans should not be restricted to the sectors.

o   Cross-cutting issues such as unpaid work, land and asset entitlements, skill development and vocational training, child care, occupational heath, wages, violence against women, etc. should be mainstreamed across the implementing agencies.

o   The action plan should be made time bound and a system of accountability for each component or action point should be clearly laid down. Different deadlines may be set for different components.

o   Since the plans of action are a government commitment to the women of the country, all implementing agencies should be made accountable for its successful implementation, in the spirit of collective responsibility.

o   Appointments to the National and State Commissions for Women should be made on the recommendations of a search committee comprising of eminent individuals from every walk of life, including women's development. The search committee should be set up by a decision of the cabinet. The statutorily laid down systems for making appointments to other high level commissions and bodies can also be looked at.

o   All state commissions should have a statutory base, ensuring their legal status.

o   Resource centres for women should be set up at state levels and these centres both at the National and State levels should have more functional and financial autonomy.

o   Resource centres for women should be set up at state levels and these centres both at the National and State levels should be linked with the women's study centres.

o   Keeping in view the availability of resources and the need to deliver on commitments, MWCD should make synergistic use of the gender responsive budgeting and gender mainstreaming processes.

o   The building of budgets from below is a paradigm that can be attempted, in the spirit of devolution and democratic decentralization process.

o   The new Ministry of Women and Child Development must be suitably strengthened. Besides the competencies of gender and economics, the ministry must also have competencies in gender & trade and legal matters.

o   In view of the vision of the government to ensure the holistic and integrated empowerment of women using the tools of gender mainstreaming and gender responsive budgeting, the MWCD must have a stronger coordinating and monitoring role – being a kind of watchdog on behalf of the government, on gender issues.

o   The MWCD should take the lead in creating and maintaining a comprehensive database, for quantitative and qualitative data. The purpose would be:

1.   to base new initiatives on facts and figures,

2.   assess the gender impact of programmes and

3.   assess the level of women's participation and involvement in the planning, implementing and managing of programmes.

o   A qualitative assessment of ongoing gender sensitization programmes for government officials being undertaken by different institutions should be carried out by MWCD, with the involvement of women's groups re-structured outcome oriented gender sensitization programmes. They must be a constant and recurring phenomena for all government officials, at all levels.

o   The parliamentary committee on women's empowerment should clear all legislations before they are presented to parliament for enactment.

o   At the state and district level, the existing institutions including departments and women's commissions should be strengthened both with human and financial resources and powers.

o   At the grassroots level women's groups should be helped to federate as registered societies at panchayat and municipal level.

Schemes of the Ministry of Women and Child Development

The **Ministry of Women and Child Development**, as the nodal agency for all matters pertaining to welfare, development and empowerment of women, has evolved schemes and programmers for their benefit. These schemes are spread across a broader spectrum such as women's need for shelter, security, safety, legal aid, justice, information, maternal health, food, nutrition, etc as well as the need for economic sustenance through skill development, education and access to credit and marketing.

The schemes of the ministry like **swashakti, swayamsidha, STEP** and **swawlamban** enable economic empowerment. Working women hostels and crèches provide support services. Swadhar and short stay homes provide protection and rehabilitation to women in difficult circumstances. The ministry also supports autonomous bodies like national commission, central social welfare and development of women. These schemes were run in the tenth plan. It is proposed to continue some in the eleventh plan and also to take up new schemes. Scheme wise details are given in the following sections.

Schemes for Economic Empowerment

Swa-Shakti

The project jointly funded by IFAD, World Bank and the Government of India was launched in October 1999 and culminated on 30th June, 2005. The objective of the program was to bring out socio-economic development and empowerment of women through promotion of women SHGs, micro-credit and income-generating activities.

Swayamsiddha

This is an integrated scheme for women empowerment through formation of self help groups launched in February, 2001. The long term objective of the programme is holistic empowerment of women through a sustained process of mobilization and convergence of all the ongoing sector programmes by improving access of women to micro credit, economic resources, etc. This is a **Centrally Sponsored Scheme.** The scheme has been able to provide a forum for women empowerment, collective reflection and united action. The scheme is expected to culminate in March 2007.

It is proposed to take up **Swayamsidha** with a wider scope during the Eleventh Plan. It is also proposed to implement a women empowerment and livelihood project in four districts of Uttar Pradesh and two districts of Bihar with assistance from IFAD. The schemes of **Swayamsiddha** and **Swa- Shakti** would be merged and implemented as **Swayamsiddha**.

The Midterm Appraisal Report of the Tenth Plan has also recommended merger of these two schemes as these have similar objectives. The next phase would be a country wide programme with a larger coverage in states lagging behind on women development indices. Convergence is the basic concept in **Swayamsiddha.** The lessons learnt in Swayamsiddha and Swa-Shakti would be incorporated in the universalized Swayamsiddha giving an integrated set of training inputs in traditional and non- traditional sectors.

Swawlamban Programme

Swawlamban Programme previously known as **Women's Economic Programme** was launched in 1982-83 with assistance from the Norwegian Agency for Development Corporation . The objective of the programme is to provide training and skills to women to facilitate them to obtain employment or self-employment on a sustained basis. The target groups under the scheme are the poor and needy women, women from weaker sections of the society such as scheduled castes and scheduled tribes, etc. In order to ensure more effective implementation and for better monitoring of the scheme, it has been transferred to the state governments form 1st April 2006 with the approval of the Planning Commission.

Support to Training and Employment Program

This program seeks to provide skills and new knowledge to the poor and assetless women in the traditional sectors. Under this project, women beneficiaries are organized into viable and cohesive groups or cooperatives. A comprehensive package of services such as health care, elementary education, crèche facility, market linkages, etc. are provided besides, access to credit. Skill development is provided in ten traditional skills amongst women. This is a Central Scheme launched in 1987. The ministry is at present getting the program evaluated. Based on the results of the evaluation, the scheme is proposed to be revamped. Further, the possibilities of providing training and skills to women both in traditional and non-traditional sectors and integrating with Rashtriya Mahila Kosh for credit linkages are being considered.

Construction of Working Women Hostels

Under the scheme, financial assistance is provided to NGOs. Cooperative bodies and other agencies for construction and renting of building for working women hostels with day care centre for children to provide them safe and affordable accommodation.

This is a central scheme. The utilization of funds under the scheme has been unsatisfactory during the Tenth Plan period because NGOs are not able to avail funds due to strict norms of funding and lack of suitable proposals from the organizations.

The norms and financial pattern of assistance discourages the NGOs for construction of these hostels. At present, the norms are:

1.   Availability of land in prime location so that they get sufficient number of working women,

2.   50% of the cost of land and 25% of the cost of construction has to be borne by the NGO,

3.   Construction of the hostel is required to be completed within two years, etc. Another issue needing review is the fixed percentage of trainees and students as a proportion to working women that is uniformly applicable across the country.

4.   There should be some flexibility especially for educationally backward states and regions, where rural girls are not able to find suitable accommodation when entering the portals of higher education.

This scheme is one of the oldest programmes of the Ministry. But as now only 873 hostels have been constructed under the scheme. With the increasing number of working women, the need for adequate housing and shelter for working women is now felt not only in big cities but also in small towns and rural areas. Hence, a Committee to revamp the scheme has been set-up under the chairpersonship of Secretary, Ministry of Women and Child Development to make the scheme more viable and to avail of the funds due to escalating costs of land.

The possibility of approaching the land and development authorities for allocating land for working women hostels in their states is also being considered. Construction would be taken up by the ministers in charge of women's affairs and the constructed building handed over to an NGO for running the hostel. Recurring grants for maintenance would be given to NGOs. Then monitoring also would be easier unlike in the present scheme where once the construction is over, the ministry has no control over the NGOs.

In the current scheme, a day care centre is optional. Women with small children would not prefer to stay in the hostel if the hostel does not have a day care centre attached to it. The Committee would look into this aspect

     THE POWER OF WOMEN

as well. In view of these, it is proposed to totally revamp the scheme and the revamped scheme would be run in the XI plan.

Relief, Protection and Rehabilitation to Women in Difficult Circumstances

Swadhar

o   This scheme was launched in 2001-02 for providing relief and rehabilitation to women in difficult circumstances. The main objectives of the scheme are as follows:

o   This provides primary need of shelter, food, clothing and care to the marginalized women and girls living in difficult circumstances who are without any social and economic support.

o   To provide emotional support and counselling to women.

o   To rehabilitate destitute women socially and economically through education, awareness, skill upgradation and personality development.

o   To arrange for specific clinical, legal and other support for women in need of those interventions by linking and networking with other organisation in both government and non- government sectors on case to case basis.

o   To provide helpline or other facilities.

Beneficiaries covered under the scheme are widows deserted by their families, women prisoners released from jail, women survivors of natural disaster, trafficked women, women victims of violence, and mentally challenged women.

The number of homes currently functional in our country is grossly inadequate. The requirements of women being catered to by the scheme are different. The needs of mentally challenged women are quite different from that of women rescued from trafficking or women survivors of disasters. Hence, it is proposed to set up different homes for women with different needs. The recently introduced protection of women from domestic violence act provides that women seeking shelter should be accommodated in the shelter homes. These call for increase in the number of shelter homes in the country. In the XI Plan, it is proposed to set up one home in each district. It is also proposed to revise the schematic norms.

The root cause of most of these problems being faced by women is lack of economic independence among women. Providing training and skills in various vocations to women living in shelter homes will facilitate them to obtain employment on a sustained basis. Though the scheme in the current form provides for vocational training, no separate funds are being provided for the purpose. Organisations are expected to seek convergence of the benefits of schemes like **STEP. Swawlamban,** etc. In the XL Plan, it is proposed to allocate funds for vocational training to the women . It is also proposed to revise the norms for food, medical expenses, clothing, rent , etc under the scheme.

Compensation to Rape Victims

The Hon'ble Supreme Court in **Delhi Domestic Working Women's Forum Vs. Union of India** and others writ petition had directed the National Commission for Women to evolve a "scheme so as to wipe out the tears of unfortunate victims." The Supreme Court observed that having regard to the Directive Principles contained in the article of the Constitution, it was necessary to set up criminal Injuries Compensation Board, as victims besides the mental anguish, frequently incur substantial financial loss and in some cases are too traumatized to continue in employment. The Court further directed that compensation for victims will be awarded by the court on conviction of the offender and by the criminal injuries compensation board whether or not a conviction has taken place. The board shall take into account pain, suffering and shock as well as loss of earnings due to pregnancy and the expenses of child birth if this occurs as a result.

Accordingly NCW has drafted a scheme titled, "Relief to and Rehabilitation of Victims." It is proposed to initiate the scheme in the XI Plan. The budgetary requirements for the scheme in the XI Plan, is estimated.

Pilot Projects for women in difficult circumstances

The schemes that are being run for women look at women as one homogenous group. In reality, there are different categories of women requiring different interventions. In the Introductory of this report, vulnerable women have been grouped into different types.

Implementation of Protection from Domestic Violence Act and other Acts of the Ministry

The protection of women from domestic violence act came into force on 26th October, 2006. In the XI Plan it is proposed to take up the following for effective implementation of the PWDDVA.

- Set up the required infrastructure and requirements to make the act effective.

- Provide training, sensitization and capacity building of protection offers, service providers, members of the judiciary, police, medical professionals, counsellors, lawyers, etc on the issue of domestic violence and the use of law to redress the same.

- Monitoring the appointment of protection officers by regular feedback from the various states.

- Set up effective MIS to monitor its implementation.

- Give wide publicity to the Act.

The Ministry is in the process of drafting an act to prevent workplace. It is proposed to allocate for implementation of this and other acts that the Ministry may bring into force during the XI Plan.

Research and Evaluation

Ensuring efficient implementation of policies and programmes is the most important aspect of any intervention. The tools and strategies to assess these aspects are research, monitoring and evaluation. Considering the importance and the necessity of research, monitoring and evaluation of all policies and programmes, the Ministry of Women and Child Development is operating a GIA scheme for research, monitoring and evaluation.

During the plan in order to give more thrust to the development of women and children, many new schemes such as Integrated Child Protection Scheme, SwayamSidhHa, over hauling, rationalization and expansion of already running schemes such as ICDS are being conceived of. New acts and rules, amendment of existing rules and regulations, may also be brought out. The working of Domestic Violence Act 2005 and its rules recently notified need to be assessed for remedial actions; the outcomes and outputs are to be matched with outlays and the directions of the interventions are to be altered if necessary. It is proposed to include the following areas for research, monitoring, evaluation and publication during the plan.

- Prevention of Female Foeticide/Infanticide

- Working of Prohibition of Child Marriage Act

- Issues relating to child, Pilgrim tourism, Tourism

- Studies on children of prostitutes

- Workshop seminars on spreading awareness about ITPA act, ill effectS of foeticide and infanticide, child marriage, etc.

- Awareness campaigns for the police and other enforcement authorities implementing officials of acts and rules

- Concurrent monitoring evaluation of schemes

- Development of databases on women and children

- Preparation of child development index

- Create mappings showing comparative status of women and children in different states and UTs

- Creation of directory of facilities created under various welfare schemes

- Information booklets and brochures to propagate the schemes of Govt. of India WCD for women and children

- Statistical publications on women and children

- In case of ICDS scheme workshops on district level awareness of ICDS in selected areas where the malnutrition is highly prevalent

- Working of existing acts for women and children, etc

- All India surveys impact studies evaluation on various issues and schemes pertaining to women and children

- Undertake the research, evaluation, monitoring and publication activities during the Eleventh five year plan, plan outlay of rupees proposed.

Monitoring and evaluation of the progress made in improving the status of women is extremely important, systems should be in place for regular monitoring and evaluation of all gender development indicators may be compiled at all India, State and District levels and disseminated widely for use by the policy makers, planners and programme implementation authorities. Further analytical studies may be undertaken to bring out regional imbalances for enabling corrective action. Hence, a cell for development of statistical databases on women and child and other related issues may be set up, which may undertake the following important activities.

Statistical publications on women and children/creation and maintenance of database of important parameters on women and children to reflect the progress by comparative analysis.

Compilation of GDI/GEM and publication of India country report with annual periodicity, development of statistical data on emerging topics such as violence against women, feminization of poverty etc, identify gender related data gaps and organize sample surveys by reputed government AND non government agencies to fill up the data gaps and to monitor implementation of policies and programmes of other tasks entrusted to WCD.

Autonomous Organisations under MWCD

Rashtriya Mahila Kosh

RMK was established in 1993 to provide micro credit in a quasi formal manner to the poor women for income generating, production, skill development and housing activities in order to make them economically independent. RMK mainly channelizes its support through NGOs, voluntary agencies, States Women Development Corporations, Co-operative societies, state government agencies, Urban Women Co-op Banks, etc. to the women SHGs. It was started with an initial corpus which has been recycled to reach cumulative sanctions of loans. It has maintained a high recovery rate of over 90%.

- RMK would be the nodal agency body for micro credit for women.

- RMK would act as the premier advocacy organisation for the development of micro finance sector at national and international level to enhance the flow of micro-credit in the unorganised sector for women.

- Mechanism would be evolved to access credit from RMK for women SHGs instead of banks as an alternative financial institution by all ministries which are,   promoting implementing subsidy linked SHG programmes. To this end, institutional capacity of RMK should be expanded through organizational expansion by providing adequate financial support complemented with socio, political and economic inputs. Also, with the universalized Swayamsidhha in the 11th Plan, RMK is required to be expanded.

- RMK would expand its role from a mere credit disbursal agency to a genuine community based, women oriented, saving cum lending agency.

Central Social Welfare Board

CSWB was set up on 12th August, 1953 by a Resolution of Govt. of India to act as an apex body at National level for welfare and development of women and children. State Social Welfare Boards were established in 1954 in all State capitals to support CSWB in achieving its objectives.

It is proposed to review all the existing schemes and restructure them looking into the current requirements. Programmes of CSWB would be merged with those of the Ministry like the scheme on Short Homes and Working Women Hostels. New schemes if need be taken up and the scheme like condensed courses of education for women would be modified during the XI Plan.

There is a strong case for restructuring of the CSWD and the State Social Welfare Advisory Boards to meet the needs of development of women and children in the fast changing economic scenario. The State Boards in particular need to be more responsive and in tune with requirements in areas.

Family Counselling Centres

Objectives

- Counselling and rehabilitative services for women & families affected by domestic violence, marital discord or family maladjustment.
- Pre-marital counselling for preparing youth for healthy interpersonal relationships, responsible parenthood and strengthening the institution of family.

Vision for the XI Plan

- The programme would be expanded to respond to felt needs of the society.
- More impetus on training and orientation of counsellors to provide professional services and strengthening of the scheme through capacity building of voluntary organisations.
- To enlarge the coverage in a phased manner so that every district has at least two FCCs.
- To give wide publicity to the scheme and networking with other stakeholders for settlement of cases.

Short Stay Homes

Objectives

- Women and their minor children, in difficult circumstances are provided comprehensive institutionalised services such as shelter, counselling, vocational training and rehabilitation for a period of 6 months to 3 years.

Condensed Course of Education for Women

Objectives

- Providing education to adolescent girls and women who are school dropouts or did not have opportunity of joining formal education system to pass primary middle level examination with inputs skill development.

- Scope of curriculum of all courses to be enlarged to include component of like skills, social skills and negotiating skills.

- To enhance intensity and impact of the scheme by reorientation, duration and time of the courses and to incorporate provision for educational tours, crèches and nutrition in the scheme.

- Schematic pattern of the scheme to be revised.

Rajiv Gandhi National Creche Scheme for the Children of Working Mothers

Objectives

- Working women from the economically weaker sections are provided support services in terms of substitute care through crèches for children in the age group of 0-6 years. They are provided day care services, supplementary nutrition, health care services and early childhood education.

Awareness Generation Programme

Objectives

- Camps are organized in the community for generating awareness among masses on issues relating to status, legal rights, problem of women and other social issues.

- To create an enabling environment for effective participation of women in decision making process and for asserting their social, economic and political rights.

Vision for the XI Plan

- Regular campaign on issues such as female foeticide, physical abuse, trafficking, gender discrimination and domestic violence may be organized.

- To develop audio-visual and print material in local language/ dialect for dissemination of information during the camps

- Duration of camps may be made flexible.

- Organization of special camps for school children, college students on stress management, family life education, self defence and personality development.

Working Women Hostel

Under this scheme, CSWB provides maintenance grants to those working women hostels which have not been constructed with assistance from the Ministry of Women and Child Development. The maintenance grant is restricted for a period of five years.

- The schematic norms need to be revised.

- The schemes of the Board and the Ministry would be merged.

National Commission for Women

The National Commission for Women was set up in 1992 to protect and safeguard the rights of women. The activities of the Commission include receiving complaints or **suo moto** enquiring in cases of deprivation of rights of women, providing counselling, conducting **Parivarik Lok Adalats** and awareness programmes and organizing public hearings.

The National Commission for Women being the nodal agency for protection of the rights of women needs to be strengthened. The NCW act needs to be suitably amended to give the Commission more power.

Investing in the Power of Women

Introduction

Women around the world have been starting business at staggering rates. Data from the **Global Entrepreneurship Monitor Women's Report** shows that an estimated 126 million women were starting or running business in 67 economies across the globe. A predicted five million women owners in these economies plan to grow their business by at least six employees over the next five years. In many developing nations, these businesses are the sole means of support for poor families. At the same time, women's entrepreneurship rates differ around the world, as do their impact on job creation and innovation, and, globally, the start up and growth rates of women entrepreneurs are lower than those of men. Generally, women entrepreneurs start their businesses out of necessity, needing the income to support their families, rather than to pursue a particular business opportunity. Women are also somewhat more likely to operate businesses as a single founder without employees.

The global gender gap between men's and women's rates of and approaches to entrepreneurship is problematic for economies that need all entrepreneurs to contribute to their growth and overall welfare.

Entrepreneurship is increasingly recognized as a broad based driver of economic growth and societal well being. For women who are primary caregivers, entrepreneurship also offers a means to better support their families. While around the world efforts to advance women's entrepreneurship vary, training and business education are sometimes offered as a solution for closing this gender gap by directly supporting the growth of women owned firms, particularly smaller emerging firms. In some countries, such as Taiwan, Korea and Chile, programmes for women entrepreneurs are sponsored by national governments, and focus on helping women access financing. Ireland uses a different approach by matching female role models to early stage entrepreneurship. These programmes and others sow that entrepreneurship education can increase women's self-confidence in their entrepreneurial ventures. However, these programmes are generally quite small and highly regionalized with many variations across economies and cultures.

More specifically, institutional and contextual factors such as laws, norms, regulations and religion as well as social networks, family roles and cultural expectations influence the ways in which women start and grow their ventures.

These factors work at both the macro and micro level. From a macro perspective, developing countries tend to have larger gender gaps in terms of both economic equality and workforce participation levels. "From a more micro point of view, women around the world tend to have less confidence in those places where they do report being more confident, women are more likely to engage and succeed in entrepreneurship.

The wide variations around the world in these institutional, social and cultural factors present significant needs in developing a universal training programme, one that takes into account contextual needs, while at the same time provides a set of widely applicable entrepreneurial business skills. Even though there may be differences in culture, social and regulatory environments across countries, the fact remains that there are general similarities in terms of the basic business education needs that women have, especially when it comes to growing ventures. More specifically, growth oriented women need education in basic entrepreneurship and business practices, approaches to financing, leadership skills and growth strategies, as well as mentorship and advising support through their growth process.

The **Goldman Sachs 10,000 women initiative** is the first to address these needs with a global effort. Although it remains a challenge to deliver local, customized support, 10,000 women demonstrates that a standardized approach, coupled with local mentoring and networking assistance, can make a significant difference in helping women entrepreneurs grow their businesses. This report presents an analysis of the data collected over the first four years of the initiative, and suggests how and why supports for women entrepreneurs can impact the trajectory of economies and whole societies. The analysis builds on the results of an independent assessment of 10,000 women in India, conducted by the International Centre for Research on Women, a leading institution in the field of women's empowerment.

The women entrepreneurs attributed improved business practices and increased confidence to their participation in the programme. Our analysis shows similar results not only in India, but across the portfolio of 10,000 women countries.

The Goldman Sachs 10,000 Women Initiative

- Educated 10,000 women

- Focus on underserved women SME owners

- Partner with local academic institutions to build capacity in the selected countries.

- Rigorously measure results

The Goldman Sachs Foundation identified specific emerging markets in which the initiative could best achieve its goal of spurring economic growth and job creation by connecting resources to those women entrepreneurs most in need of support. This resulted in the selection of fast growing countries such as Brazil, India and China, as well as nations like Afghanistan and Liberia that are in an earlier stage of economic growth and development. In all cases, the following criteria:

- Presence of strong partner institution

- Recent improvement in the enabling environment for women entrepreneurs

- Economic development need

- Population size/scalability

With their local partners in each country, 10,000 women created certificate programmes that provide an average of 180 hours of classroom instruction over a period ranging from five weeks to six months. Courses include marketing, accounting, business plan writing, strategic planning and e-commerce, among others. Each programme trains local women whose financial and practical circumstances would normally prevent them from receiving a traditional business education. The participants receive a comprehensive package of business training and support that is tailored to the local context and typically includes mentoring, business advising and, in select countries, links to capital.

The first 10,000 women partnership was launched at Pan Atlantic University in Nigeria and graduated its first cohort of 23 women entrepreneurs in September 2008. Five years later, the initiative has reached 10,000 women n 43 countries through partnership with 89 academic and non- profit instructions.

Core Curriculum

Local academic partners were paired with leading global business schools to create the curricula for their respective programs and provide faculty exchange opportunities and training. Despite being developed separately, the resultant curricula were quite similar in content, although there was some allowance for the customization of delivery methods, the amount of time spent on certain topics, and the overall program length based on the country context.

The pairing of academic institutions to develop and deliver the curriculum was part of a larger institutional capacity building effort that also extended to program monitoring and evaluation. Development of the M&E process was viewed as an opportunity to build a new generation of local experts who could implement measurement for continuous program improvement, as well as apply what they had learned to other local, mission driven endeavors. To this end, the foundation funded a full time, dedicated representative at each location, referred to as an M&E liaison, focused exclusively on coordinating data gathering and validation.

Who are the 10,000 Women Entrepreneurs?

Entrepreneur Profile

The 10,000 women represent more than 40 nationalities. The majority of participants graduated from core programs managed directly by the Goldman Sachs Foundation in 15 countries. In addition, a small minority graduated from partner programs created for the express purpose of bringing 10,000 women to a broader audience. These partnerships included the U.S. Department of State Global Cohorts Program, Room to Read and CAMFED international, among others.

The profile of the 10,000 women graduated from core programs managed directly by the **Goldman Sachs Foundation** in 15 countries. And women graduate is characterized by her education, material status, household size and age.

Although there are many differences among the participants, considering the averages within the program provides a starting point for understanding the typical woman business owner. Most had at least some tertiary education, but did not possess a college degree, participants from Egypt and Nigeria tended to be more highly educated respectively, with at least some college, while less than 25% of the women in Rwanda and Kenya had any college education.

Most participants are between 35 and 45 years old and married. They manage household averaging 3.7 people and also support an average of 1.9 dependents outside their household.

Business Profile

The 10,000 women participants had an average of five years of experience in business ownership across 15 different industries. The highest percentage of women, were engaged in "other services," which included education lessons, home services and personal services. Other top industries were food and beverages with textiles and clothing . Together, these three industries represent program participants. Not surprisingly, there was a wide variation by country. For instance, India, South Africa, Rwanda and Peru had higher than average numbers of women in other services, while in Mexico participants were involved in textiles and clothing.

Participants with at least some college were more likely to run businesses in media services, technology and "other services." On the other hand, woman without some college were more likely to own a business in the more highly competitive consumer services or retail industries, which generally have lower start up costs and are much more competitive.

At the beginning of the program, women entrepreneurs were asked about the size of their businesses both in terms of number of employees and revenues. The overall average sales were, but the range of sales was quite broad, form under to more than million. Chinese women business owners averaged the highest level of revenues at, while the businesses owned by Liberian women were the smallest. As with sales, the number of employees ranged widely from under 5 to more than 1,100, with an average of 12.4 employees at entry into the program. The businesses in Liberia were the smallest while those in China were the largest. The averages show that the women selected to participate in the program already operated active businesses with significant track records of revenue and employment in their local economies.

Influences on Growth

Business growth is often strongly influenced by industry factors. Program participants in technology and leisure services grew the most in terms of both revenue and employment. Within the first six months, more than 75% of business in these sectors grew revenues. Those in technology added an average of 9.8 jobs, while those in leisure services added one employee. At 18 months, those in transportation and other consumer products were most likely to grow revenues, while those in other consumer products and retail were most likely to grow employment, adding an average of 11.4 and 3.2 employees, respectively.

The relationship between the education level of the women business owners and their rate of business growth is worth noting. Six months after graduation, there is no difference in their business growth by level of education. However, at 18 months those women with no college education had grown employment by, while those women with some college grew by an aggressive percent.

The program's so called wraparound services were highly valued by the participants and perceived as contributing to their growth.

These services included mentoring, business advising and networking opportunities. Only 56% participants had a business advisor or mentor when they entered the program. By six months, this figure rose which report that their mentor or business advisor was provided by 10,000 women. These relationships were highly valued by the women, responding that their mentor or advisor helped them grow their businesses. It is clear then that this type of intervention should be part of any future efforts to support women entrepreneurs.

Formal networking is another major area of change for women in this program. At baseline, only 46% reported participating in formal networking activities. This figure grew by almost 30 percentage points by six months after graduation. Most of the 10,000 women agreed or strongly agreed that networking helped grow their business. Nearly 90% reported that their growth was supposed by networking with classmates, demonstrating the power of the bonds formed by the women's experience in the program.

Personal Leadership Development

For entrepreneurs to move form start up to growth, they need to begin to think of themselves as leaders. Following the completion of the program, we see a significant rise in the development of the women's leadership skills. Participants were asked about their confidence in decision-making, negotiation and selling over the course of the program. Confidence in such skills is essential for business growth as it supports outreach to new partners, the hiring of new employees and acquiring other necessary resources. At baseline, 60% of participants rated their confidence in their decision-making abilities as effective or highly effective. Six months after graduation, this number had risen to 72%, and by 18 months it was 73%. This rise of more than 20% suggests that the attention to leadership development and practical business skill education makes a recognizable difference to the women participants.

Most women consider themselves to be effective sellers. At the start of the program, participants were confident or highly confident in their selling and communicating skills, and this rose to within six months. At 18 months, 80.5% considered themselves effective or highly effective. While these increases were across nearly all the countries, there is some variation, ranging from 66% in China to 96% in Liberia.

In negotiating with customers and suppliers, 62% of participants rated themselves effective or highly effective at baseline. This rose by nine points over six months, and continued to rise to 75% at 18 months, representing an increase of more than 20%. Country comparisons indicate that cultural factors may be at play here. In China for example, although women participants experienced some of the highest rates of growth, they reported the lowest levels of confidence in negotiations. Other research has shown Chinese women are less likely than their male counterparts to see opportunities, or believe they have the capabilities to start a business. They also rank lower on these dimensions than women from most other regions of the world. More research is required to understand the impact of culture on confidence of women entrepreneurs.

Value for the Local Community

A final key outcome for the women participants is their commitment to the local community and a strong sense of giving back to other women entrepreneurs. Most women reported "paying it forward" by mentoring and reaching skills to an average of eight other women. The fact that 90% of participants are mentoring and advising eight others is most impressive, and suggest that the participants in this survey have touched more than 20,000 additional women entrepreneurs.

And finally, we see the 10,000 women giving back through their own civic engagement. More than 20% of participants reported that they had become leaders in community groups, associations, and religious groups after graduation.

10,000 Women – A Look Across Three Continents

As developing countries on three different continents Brazil, China and Nigeria provide a view of how the program operates similarly across different contexts.

Participants reported strong revenue and job growth in all three countries, but there were significant differences in behavioural changes and business practices. In Brazil, less than half of the women reported being confident or highly confident in their ability to make difficult decisions before they started 10,000 women. By six and 18 months following their graduation, however, this figure had increased . Only 5% of participants had an operational business plan at baseline. Six months later, remarkably, the Brazilian graduates reported having an up-to-date business plan that they used in their daily operations.

For business performance, the changes are even more remarkable. By six months, the women participants from Brazil experienced revenue growth, and more than half had hired new employees. At 18 months, 72% continued to report revenue growth, and had added jobs.

Similar to Brazilian graduates, Chinese women showed significant improvement in creation and use of a business plan. While only 26% of participants in China reported having an operational business plan at the baseline, six months later, reported having an up-to- date business plan that they used in their daily operations. Interestingly, for Chinese women graduates, the percentages of family members who "very much" believe they can be a successful business woman decreased from the baseline to both 6 months and 18 months after graduation. Percentages dropped from 37% to 25%, whereas in Brazil and Nigeria, not only were these numbers higher at the baseline, at respectively, but they also remained steady over time, with reporting high confidence at 18 months.

While the perception of family support may be lower, this has not impacted business performance following graduation from the 10,000 women program in China. Six months after graduation, 70% of Chinese participants grew their revenues and, by 18 months, 80% reported revenue growth. Similarly, for employment, six months after graduating, 55% hired more employees and 73% reported hiring more employees after 18 months.

Much like the Brazilian women graduates, those in Nigeria responded with notable increase in effective decision-making from 65% in the baseline survey to 85% at 6 months and 93% at 18 months.

A 10,000 Women Graduate Linlin from China

Linlin graduated from the 10,000 women program at Beijing's Tsinghua University. She operates day care centres and kindergartens that provide educational services to children from 0-6 years of age. She applied to the program to learn how to overcome challenges in financial planning and quality control. After graduation, she has "improved my overall management skills and expertise," and the program "gave me the knowledge and confidence that I needed to apply for a bank loan."

Linlin's workforce has grown to more than 100, from just four employees in 2011. Her relationships with more than 300 clients have allowed her to more than triple her revenues. She also started a 10,000 women alumni club in Beijing. Through this platform, she organizes events for fellow classmates where they can "share both professional and personal challenges and solutions and become the best supporting force for each other as women entrepreneurs."

Since graduation, her future goals have changed as well. She credits the program with making her more "brave and confident." Her short term goal is "to open another 10 directly managed community day care centres in Beijing and in five other cities through co-investment." Longer term she wants to open an additional 50 centre of her own, and another 50 co-invested community day care centres and kindergartens in Beijing and beyond. Eventually, she says, "I hope to become a leader in preschool education in both commercial operations and academic research."

How do the 10,000 Women Entrepreneurs Develop Business Practices for Growth?

There are a variety of key business practices that can support business growth. For 10,000 women, these included the use of a business plan, the ability to pitch that plan and general marketing and financial management practices.

Business Plans

At the start of the program, most participants did not have a written business plan, and only had an up-to-date business plan that guided their daily work. The usage of business plans varied considerably by country at baseline. For example, in Turkey, had a current business plan compared with in Brazil, not only to business plans guide daily decision making in the business, they also play a role in securing external debt and equity financing. It is critical to note that the percentage of women with up-to-date operational business plans more than tripled to within six months after graduation.

There are similar findings for business plan presentations, which can be an important factor in obtaining external financing. At the beginning of the program, very less graduates had participated in business plan presentations over the prior 12 months. Of those that did, agreed or strongly agreed that doing so helped grow their business. At six months, the participation rate in such events more than doubled to graduates, and of these, presented in at least one such event organized by 10,000 women. Over 40% participated in business plan presentations, which means that many women are seeking and finding similar opportunities outside of the program. Of those that had participated in any business plan presentation, agreed or strongly agreed that doing so had helped grow their business.

Market Approach

Many women grew their businesses by changing their approaches to their markets. Some developed new products, improved the quality of existing products, or discontinued an unprofitable product. Others changed their market reach by opening or closing a location, partnered with another organization, or started to export. By 18 months, the percentage of participants reported that they had stopped selling unprofitable products and services that had nearly doubled and the percentage reporting that they had not made any changes was reduced to less than half of the baseline percentage.

These responses indicate that the women participants are pruning product lines and focusing efforts in specific locations that would, in effect, increase efficiencies in their businesses.

The program's emphasis on finance and accounting helps the women understand the value of business statements.

Financial Business

A key business practice contributing to business growth is the women's understanding and use of budgets and other formal financial statements, specifically income, cash follow and balance sheet statements. At the beginning of the program, participants used 1.4 of these tools out of the four, but notably, more than 20% reported not using any financial statements at all. The most common financial statement tool graduates used was cash flow statements, followed by income statements, followed by income statements, balance sheets and budgets. At six months, the use of all financial statements had measurably increased. Participants reported a nearly 10% increase in the use of cash flow and income statements, an 8% increase in the use of balance sheets and a nearly 13% increase in the use of budgets. Overall, those using some form of financial statement increased by 18%. These results suggest that the program's emphasis on finance and accounting helps the women understand the value of these statements, and establish a platform for growth. For example, in order to apply for any external financing, entrepreneurs must have such documents prepared and available. Participants who used financial statements were most likely to apply for funding and receive approval. For example, at six months, business owners that use cash flow statements receive approval for their funding applications of the time as opposed to those that don't.

Access to Capital: A Key Growth Challenge

Although participants succeeded in improving their overall financial statements, one area where they continued to struggle was in accessing capital. 10,000 women graduates tend to self-finance their growth by reinvesting the capital generated by the business. In fact, less than a third of participants had received funding from a financial institution, and just 47% had even applied at some point, either before or participating in the program. While the majority of participants do not apply for financing, those who do typically received approval for their loans. The high approval rates suggest that these women are largely creditworthy. So why are they not pursuing external funding?

Many might be quick to assume that women don't apply for capital because they don't have a need for it. But studies show that, in most countries, women have a greater credit need than men, and are less likely to receive loans due to gender stereotypes. Moreover, the IFC has reported that among SME lenders in emerging markets, women represent a small minority of borrowers. This pattern is also seen in 10,000 women. Of the 60% of the women who have not applied for external funding, roughly 50% reported at baseline that they actually have a need, but did not apply for other reasons, including unattractive loan terms, too high a risk, not understanding how to apply, overly complex procedures, high levels of security and collateral required and a lack of confidence about the likelihood of being approved. These generally negative perceptions about the likelihood of successfully acquiring funding may be deterring women from applying. It is likely to say that they didn't understand how to apply or that they feared they would be rejected. These changes suggest a new level of understanding and awareness, likely attributable to the 10,000 women curriculum, which focuses specially on finance and accounting. The curriculum does not, however, include modules detailing specifically how to apply for external funding, which may help to explain why the rates of application do not increase following graduation from the program. Because the majority of 10,000 women businesses are growing without outside funding, it is possible that the businesses are not achieving their full growth potential or that funding needs are met for current rates of growth. We can only speculate as to the growth rates in terms of revenues and employees that might be achieved with the investment of external capital.

A deeper analysis of the women who did not seek external capital shows that they funded their ventures with their own personal money, with an additional 21.8% using funds from family and friends. Women investing their own money into their businesses are more likely to apply for outside funding, and those actually applying for funding are more likely to receive funding from family and friends. Such trends might be related to personal commitment, or what is referred to as "skin in the game," in that a personal financial investment puts the entrepreneur more at financial risk, and therefore she might wish to hedge her risk by either applying for outside funding, or by requesting funds from family and friends. At the same time, others may be more confident in providing funds when they see the business owner also investing in herself.

A 10,000 Women Graduate Ayo from Nigeria

Ayo delivers motivational speeches throughout Nigeria, hoping "to promote the principle of self- worth and self-reliance. I believe that when this mindset is in place, our national development, growth and prosperity is only a matter of time."

Ayo founded her catering business in Lagos, Nigeria, with just $8 USD. Initially, her customers were friends and family members. However, as her business expanded to provide meals in private homes and officers, she struggled with the basic challenges of record keeping, managing people and marketing her services to new clients. She recognized that she needed management skills to continue to grow her business.

Through the 10,000 women program, Ayo learned how to better manage her cash flow, to identify her target segment in the market and to communicate her unique value proposition to customers. She built strategic partnerships, opened a restaurant and has since taken over an entire building in order to run her business more efficiently. She manages a full time staff of 12 employees, and for larger jobs, her business creates more employment opportunities for as many as 30 part time workers. Ayo has seen her revenue grow thirty fold since graduating from 10,000 women in 2008, and her aspiration for her business to become a household name in Logos has come closer to reality.

Ayo has enrolled in an MBA program, and is utilizing social and print media to reach new clients. In addition to her business success, Ayo has credited the program with building her confidence.

"I feel I can go anywhere. My daughter sees me as her hero. She says I am strong." And her husband has said, "Our lives have been turned around. I knew she would achieve something, but I didn't know it would be at this scale."

Ayo has become a role model young women and men alike. Her creativity, determination and resilience have inspired many young women who lacked the confidence to follow their person. Ayo's goal is "to be able to reach out to as many people as possible." She holds weekly mentoring sessions for women entrepreneurs at her business, and is helping them realize their potential.

Conclusions and Implications

In 2013, the 10,000 women initiative achieved its goal of providing business and management education to 10,000 underserved women around the world. The results of this first comprehensive analysis show that these women, who might not qualify for other types of programs due to their financial and practical circumstances, have achieved significant business growth and personal leadership development. Through mentoring, advising and hours of basic business skills training, the 10,000 women graduates gained confidence, grew their businesses in sales and employees and are strengthening their communities by mentoring other women.

Not only does the 10,000 women program reflect the aggregate effect of similar training across multiple cohorts and countries, but we also see where there are particular differences that suggest new possibilities for training. The analysis of Brazil, China and Nigeria demonstrates how cultural factors make a difference in women's development of self-confidence in business decision-making and selling, as well as the amount of family support of women entrepreneurs.

There are four key conclusions that we can draw from our analysis of the data set emerging out of Goldman Sachs Foundation's experience in implementing 10,000 women over the past five years.

1.   Women can be exceptional entrepreneurs across a diverse array of country and cultural contexts

Women entrepreneurs participating in the 10,000 women program are exceptional in two main ways. First, as a result of their participation, they grew their businesses dramatically in terms of sales and employees. Second, the 10,000 women achieved growth despite being generally less educated and having significantly more household responsibilities. Most are managing households with an average of 3.7 members while also supporting an average of two additional dependents in the household. That these women grew their education level and family responsibilities is a significant testament to their perseverance, and the ability to overcome challenges that their male counterparts do not face.

2.   10,000 women helps entrepreneurs grow their businesses and develop their business acumen

The business training and support provided by 10,000 women enables entrepreneurs to increase their revenues and hire more employees. Although the percentage growth is in part due to the fact that these firms are generally small, this growth was recognized almost immediately after graduation, and continued over time at an impressive rate. The evidence that these women increased their use of business plans and adjusted their product lines suggest they gained efficiencies in their businesses that translated directly to the bottom line. The women's confidence in their leadership skills rose significantly as well. Several studies show that lack of confidence limits growth expectations and actual business performance, so this program makes a large step forward by providing the mentoring training and skills that lead to increased confidence.

3.   Mentoring, advising and networks are highly valued in the growth process

Some 89% of participants agreed or strongly agreed that having a mentor or business advisor helped them grow their businesses. Similar results were observed for networking with classmates, especially face-to-face. Because women's networks are often smaller and less diverse than those of their male counterparts, 10,000 women provide a key resource for goal-oriented women entrepreneurs. Perhaps inspired by their experience in the program, 90% of participants "pay it forward" by mentoring and teaching business skills to an average of eight other women in their communities. This implies that more than 70,000 women will be touched by this initiative.

4. Women entrepreneurs grow their businesses despite a lack of external financing

10,000 women graduates achieve high rates of growth, but tend to finance this growth through retained earnings and internal sources. Our analysis shows that growth oriented women entrepreneurs need external capital but usually do not apply for it. Participants cited barriers such as unfavourable loan terms and collateral requirements, risk aversion and complexity of the application process. Among those that apply for external funding, however, a majority are approved, demonstrating that female entrepreneurs like the 10,000 women graduates are creditworthy. While it is true that the 10,000 women have achieved growth this far, this analysis begs the question of whether they could be more successful if they had greater access to outside funding.

Entrepreneurship is increasingly recognized as a broad-based driver of economic growth and societal well-being.

Segment represent, and better market its services to this segment. On the demand side, further interventions are required to educate women about available financing options and ensure that they have the skills necessary to obtain the financing that meets their specific needs.

• Success of women only programs

The significant improvement in leadership skills and confidence suggests that women only programs can be quite effective in the development of female entrepreneurial talent. These entrepreneurs are exceptional role models for other women in their countries, in that they do not fit the stereotype of growth oriented entrepreneurs. Therefore, they should be showcased by the media, in educational teaching materials and in other ways so as to inspire the next generation of women entrepreneurs.

• Need to scale

The success of the 10,000 women initiative suggests that this type of training, education and wraparound support should be made available to other countries and populations of growth oriented women entrepreneurs.

Developing trainers and business advisors, scaling similar initiatives, as well as utilization of technology for alternative delivery methods present future opportunities.

Entrepreneurship is increasingly recognized as a broad-based driver of economic growth and societal well-being. For women who are primary caregivers, entrepreneurship offers a means to support their families as well. Training and business education for growth oriented women entrepreneurs is a solution to closing the gender gap in employment, building more prosperous communities and enabling the growth and development of nations.

About The Study – women in the workplace is the largest study on the state of women in corporate America. In 2015, Leanin.Org and Mckinsey & Company launched the study to give companies insights and tools to advance gender diversity in the workplace. Between 2015 and 2022, over 810 companies participated in the study, and more than 400,000 people were surveyed on their workplace experiences. This year, we collected information from 333 participating organizations employing more than 12 million people, surveyed more than 400,000 employees, and conducted interviews with women of diverse identities, including women of color, LGBTQ+ women, and women with disabilities. Our 2022 report focuses on how the pandemic has changed what women want from their companies, including the growing importance of opportunity, flexibility, employee well-being, and diversity, equity, and inclusion.

Introduction

There are always winners and losers in the war for talent, and the stakes are higher than ever for companies that want to achieve gender equality.

Women are demanding more from work, and they're leaving their companies in unprecedented numbers to get it. Women leaders are switching jobs at the higher rate we've ever seen – and at a higher rate than men in leadership. This could have serious implications for companies. Women are already significantly underrepresented in leadership. For years, few women have risen through the ranks because of the "broken rung" at the first step up to manager. Now, companies are struggling to hold on to the relatively few women leaders they have. And all these dynamics are even more pronounced for women of color.

The reason women leaders are stepping away from their companies are telling. Women leaders are just as ambitious as men, but at many companies they face headwinds that make it harder to advance. They're more likely to experience belittling micro-aggressions, such as having their judgement questioned or being mistaken for someone more junior. They're doing more to support employee well-being and foster inclusion, but this critical work is spreading them thin and going mostly unrewarded. And finally, it's increasingly important to women leaders that they work for companies that prioritize flexibility, employee well-being, and diversity, equity, and inclusion.

If companies don't take action, they won't trust their women leaders: they risk losing the next generation of women leaders, too. Young women are even more ambitious, and they place a higher premium on working in an equitable, supportive, and inclusive workplace. They're watching senior women leave for better opportunities, and they're prepared to do the same.

Women in the workplace – Pipeline

Two pipeline challenges put gender equality out of reach for most companies.

Despite modest gains in representation over the last eight years, women – and especially women of color – are still dramatically underrepresented in corporate America. And this is especially true in senior leadership: only 1 in 4 C-suite leaders is woman, and only 1 in 20 is woman of color. Moreover, most companies are grappling with two pipeline problems that make achieving gender equality in their organization all but impossible:

The "broken rung" remains broken.

For the eighth consecutive year, a "broken rung" at the first step up to manager is holding women back. For every 100 men who are promoted from entry level to manager, only 87 women are promoted, and only 82 women of color are promoted.

As a result, men significantly outnumber women at the manager level, and women can never catch up. There are simply too few women to promote into senior leadership positions.

More women leaders are leaving their companies.

Now, companies have a new pipeline problem. Women leaders are leaving their companies at the highest rate in years, and the gap between women and men leaders leaving is the largest we've ever seen. Woman at the director level gets promoted to the next level, two women directors are choosing to leave their company.

The "broken rung" is still holding women back.

The biggest obstacle women face on the path to senior leadership is the first step up to manager. For every 100 men promoted from entry level to manager, only 87 women are promoted, and only 82 women of color are promoted.

As a result, men significantly outnumber women at the manager level, and women can never catch up. There are simply too few women to promote into senior leadership positions.

Women remain deeply underrepresented in technical roles declined between 2018 and 2022.

Women are far less likely than men to work in engineering and technical fields, and women's relative representation in these jobs is lower than it was in 2018. As a result, women in technical roles are twice as likely as women overall to say they are frequently the only woman in the room at work. The fact that they are so often "Only" women may partly explain why women in tech face higher rates of bias: they are more likely than women in non-technical roles to have their judgment questioned in their area of expertise and to say their gender has played a role in their being passed over for a chance to get ahead.

These trends have troubling implications for gender equality. Engineering and technical roles are among corporate America's fastest growing and highest paid job categories. If women in these roles have negative day-to-day experiences and don't see an equal path to advancement, it could lead to larger gaps in both representation and earnings between women and men overall.

Women in the workplace – Women leaders

Women leaders are demanding more from their companies, and they're increasingly willing to switch jobs to get it. Three primary factors are driving their decisions to leave.

Women leaders want to advance, but they face stronger headwinds than men.

Women leaders are as likely as men at their level to want to be promoted and aspire to senor level roles. In many companies, however, they experience micro-aggressions that undermine their authority and signal that it will be harder for them to advance.

For example, they are far more likely than men leaders to have colleagues question their judgemnt or imply that they aren't qualified for their jobs. Women leaders are also more likely to report that personal characteristics, such as their gender or being a parent, have played a role in them being denied or passed over for a raise, promotion, or chance to get ahead.

Women leaders are overworked and under recognized.

Compared to men at their level, women leaders do more to support employees well-being and foster diversity, equity, and inclusion – work that dramatically improves retention and employee satisfaction, but is not formally rewarded in most companies.

Spending time and energy on work that isn't recognized could make it harder for women leaders to advance. It also means that women leaders are stretched thinner than men in leadership; not surprisingly, women leaders are far more likely than men at their level to be burned out.

Burnout management responsibilities and unsustainable workload has made me more ambitious, but not in the same way. I'm more ambitious about going after something different. I'm more ambitious about making a career change or going after something where I feel more fulfilled.

Women leaders want a better work culture.

Women leaders are significantly more likely than men leaders to leave their jobs because they want more flexibility or because they want to work for a company that is more committed to employee well-being and diversity, equity, and inclusion. And over the last two years, these factors have only become more meaningful to women leaders.

If companies don't take action in response to these trends, they're at risk of losing more women leaders. That could have serious implications.

Compared to men at the same level, women leaders are investing more time and energy in effective people management, allyship, and DEI. They are leading the transaction to a more supportive, inclusive workplace, which is what the next generation of employees – and especially younger women – want and expect.

Companies are also at risk of losing young women.

The factors that drive women leaders to leave their companies are even more important to young women. Young women care deeply about opportunity to advance – more than two-third of women under 30 want to be senior leaders, and well over half say advancement has become more important to them in the past two years. Young women are also more likely than women leaders to say they're increasingly prioritizing flexibility and company commitment to well-being and DEI.

Companies that don't take action may struggle to recruit and retain the next generation of women leaders – and for companies that already have a "broken rung" in their leadership pipeline, this has especially worrisome implications.

Black women leaders are more ambitious than other women at their level: 59 percent of Black Women leaders want to be top executive, compared to 49 percent of women leaders overall.

But they are also more likely than women leaders of other races and ethnicities to receive signals that it will be harder for them to advance. Compared to other women at their level, Black Women leaders are more likely to have colleagues question their competence and to be subjected to demeaning behaviour – and 1 in 3 Black Women leaders say they've been denied or passed over for opportunities because of personal characteristics, including their race and gender.

Women leaders are also overworked at home.

Women at all levels are far more likely than men to be responsible for most or all of their family's housework and care-giving. But the imbalance is especially stark between men and women in leadership roles. Among entry-level employees, women are about twice as likely as men to be doing all of this work; among employees in leadership, the gap nearly doubles.

Women in the workplace – Intersectional Look

Some women face more bias and receive less support at work.

Many women experience bias not only because of their gander, but also because of their race, a disability, or other aspects of their identity – and the compounded discrimination can be much greater than the sum of its parts. As a result, these groups of women often experience more micro- aggressions and face more barriers to advancement. It's critical that companies and co-workers are aware of these dynamics so they can more effectively promote equity and inclusion for all women.

As I was progressing through my career, people kept telling me I needed to have 'executive presence.' And what they really meant was I needed to look the part. I needed to have the right clothing, I needed to look feminine enough. That was always a challenge for me, because I didn't follow the typical feminine dress code.

Although no study can fully capture the experiences of women with traditionally marginalized identities, this year's findings point to these distinct experiences.

IN THEIR WORDS

Someone I worked with went behind my back and told my VP that I was having personal conversations in Spanish on the clock. They said I wasn't working. That simply wasn't true. I was speaking Spanish on the job because I managed an entire region that was Spanish-speaking. I was so demoralized. I thought, "Why even go to work if I'm going to be bullied and harassed about the language I'm speaking?"

There have been times when I've been excluded from a work related conversation just because it's easier for other people not to have to gender me correctly. That's happened a couple times. There have been discussions within my sphere of responsibility and I know the answer, but my colleagues go around me.

Women in the workplace – Flexibility

Remote and hybrid work are game-changing for women.

Two years after the pandemic forced corporate America into a massive experiment with flexible work, enthusiasm for flexibility in all its forms is higher than ever. A vast majority of employees want to work for companies that offer remote or hybrid work options. Only 7 per cent of companies plan to pull back on remote and hybrid work in the next year, and 32 per cent say these options are likely to expand.

Although remote and hybrid won't work for all companies or all roles, it's clear that these new modes of working are here to stay. As companies continue to working they are here to stay. As companies continue to navigate this transition, there are three key things they should keep in mind.

Choice is critical.

Employees who can choose to work in the arrangement they prefer – where remote or on-site – are less burned out, happier in their jobs, and much less likely to consider leaving their companies. This points to the importance of giving employees agency and choice when possible; a one-size-fits-all approach to flexible work won't work for all employees.

The option to work remotely is especially important to women.

Only 1 in 10 women wants to work mostly on-site, and many women point to remote and hybrid work options as one of their top reasons for joining or staying with an organization, these preferences are about more than flexibility. When women work remotely at least some of the time, they experience fewer micro-aggressions and higher levels of psychological safety. The decrease in micro-aggression is especially pronounced for women of color, LGBTQ+ women, and women with disabilities – groups who typically face more demeaning and other behaviour.

Although remote and hybrid work are delivering real benefits, they may also be creating new challenges.

Most employees prefer working remotely at least some of the time. And most HR leaders say that offering flexible work options has helped diversify their talent pipelines and retain more employees from underrepresented groups. However, there are potential downsides to these new ways of working. A majority of companies are concerned that employees who work remotely feel less connected to their teams and say that remote and hybrid work are placing additional demands on managers. It's also possible that employees who primarily work from home – who are more likely to be women – will get fewer opportunities for recognition and advancement.

Employees who can choose their work arrangements are less likely to leave.

"It's important to me that my company treats people well and gives us flexibility. Those things were improving in the past, but the pandemic forced them to change faster. And now it's become a requirement to attract talent. You can't be the company that forces people to work the way you want them to work."

Women experience fewer micro-aggressions when they work remotely at least some of the time.

Some micro-aggressions just 100 percent don't happen when I'm remote. A lot of people have said, "I should be worried about not having face time, but there's another perspective, which is that people of color don't want to be in a work environment where they don't feel like they can be themselves."

Remote work options are especially critical for women with disabilities

The shift towards remote and hybrid work has been particularly beneficial for women with disabilities. Working at home can help women with disabilities be healthier and more productive, since it's easier to manage mobility issues, chronic pain, and material health conditions when you have more control over your work environment.

Women with disabilities also feel more respected and supported when they have the option to work remotely. They are less likely to experience certain micro-aggressions, such as hearing negative comments about their appearance or having colleagues openly question their qualifications. They are also more likely to say their manager trusts them to get their work done and that they feel comfortable talking openly with colleagues about their challenges.

Five steps companies can take to navigate the shift to remote and hybrid work.

For companies that are transitioning to remote and hybrid work, it's critical to ensure that these new modes of working work for everyone. This will require a mindset shift. It's not enough to tweak old policies; companies need to fundamentally rethink how work is done. To start, companies would be well served to focus their efforts in five general areas.

1. Clearly communicate plans and guidelines for flexible work

As remote and hybrid work policies continue to evolve, companies should take extra care to ensure that employees know what to expect and understand the rationale behind decisions. It's important to share guidelines about who can work remotely and why, so people don't feel they're being treated unfairly. It's also important that companies provide clear guidelines to help employees navigate the day-to-day complexities of remote and hybrid work; for example, establishing specific windows during which meetings can be scheduled and employees in different time zones are expected to be available.

2. Gather regular feedback from employees

It's hard to navigate any major transition without understanding employees' priorities and experience. But only about half of companies have surveyed employees on their preferences for remote and hybrid work over the past year – which means they may not fully understand how changes have been received. And as companies roll out new remote and hybrid work norms, they will want to keep a regular pulse on what's working for employees and what needs to be improved.

3. Invest in fostering employee connectedness

This means being international about working norms – for example, having everyone join meetings via video conference so it's easier for employees to participate when they are working remotely. It also means finding new ways to foster camaraderie and connection. Making creative use of technology to facilitate water cooler style interactions and team celebrations in a virtual work environment is a good start. Companies could also benefit from dedicating resources to team bonding events and, whether they're virtual, or in person, taking special care to make sure that all employees feel included and that events are accessible to everyone.

4. Be purposeful about in person work

Employee expectations in person work are changing – in particular, many employees don't want to come into the office to do work they can just easily do at home. In light of this, many companies are starting to refocus in person work on activities that take advantage of being together, such as high level planning, learning and development training, and bursts of heavy collaboration.

5. Make sure the playing field is level

It's important that remote and hybrid employees get the same support and opportunities as on site employees. People managers play a central role here, and many could benefit from additional training on how to foster remote and hybrid employees career development and minimize flexibility stigma. Equal access to mentorship and sponsorship are also key, yet less than half of companies offer virtual mentorship and sponsorship programs. Finally, companies can put safeguards in place to make sure employees who take advantages to remote and hybrid work options aren't disadvantaged in performance reviews.

Companies can take bolder steps to support remote and hybrid work.

"My company could do a better job of training leaders on how to manage remotely. We never had a course on how to manage remote teams. I think it's something all of our managers need, not just me."

How Blue Shield of California made a successful shift to hybrid work

Over the past two years, Blue Shield of California has made an international transaction to hybrid work, with a particular focus on balancing employees, preferences with delivering on business goals. Their approach included four key steps:

**1.	Allow remote work wherever possible.**

During the early stages of the pandemic, Blue Shield of California realized that many of their roles could be remote. Most employees now have the choice to work remotely at least some of the time, with only essential workers such as clinical staff fully on site.

**2.	Trained managers.**

More than 90 per cent of Blue Shield of California's managers completed training on how to manage hybrid teams. The training included live online workshops and tool kits on topics like supporting employee well-being and ensuring that both remote and on-site team members are included and treated fairly.

Following the training, 95 per cent of participants said they felt ready to lead in a hybrid work environment.

**3.	Make in person work purposeful.**

Blue Shield of California aligned on four types of work that are best done in person governance and planning, collaboration, connection, and learning and development.

**4.	Fostered healthy workloads.**

Blue Shield of California asked managers to work with their employees, one-on-one to create schedules that balance work and life. To protect employees, personal time, the company also has a policy of no meeting before 9 a.m. between 12 and 1 p.m. and after 5 p.m.

What impact did Blue Shield of California's programs have?

In recent employee surveys, 90 per cent of employees said the company is a great place to work, and 95 per cent of women said they felt fairly treated, in addition, Blue Shield of California appeared on **Fortune's 100 Best Companies to Work** for list in 2022, a first in the company's history.

Managers are key to retaining women – but they need more support to get this right.

Managers play an essential role in shaping women's – and all employees' – work experience. When managers invest in people management and DEI, women are happier and less burned out. They're also less likely to think about leaving their jobs and more likely to recommend their company as a good place to work – which translates to higher retention and better recruiting.

The problem is there's a growing gap between what's expected of managers and how they're being trained and rewarded. Most companies say managers have been expected to do more over the last two years to support employees' well-being and advancement and promote inclusion on their teams. At the same time, the shift to remote and hybrid work has made manager's jobs more challenging. Yet relatively few companies are adequately training managers to meet these new demands, and even fewer recognize people management and DEI efforts in manager's performance reviews. Companies are effectively treating this work as a nice to have – as opposed to a core part of a managers' job – and this disconnect is apparent in the way managers are showing up. Only about half of women say their manager regularly encourages respectful behaviour on their team, and less than half say their manager shows interest in their career and helps them manage the workload.

How companies can equip, incentivize, and reward good managers.

To begin to close the gap between what's expected of managers and how they show up, companies could benefit from focusing on two key objectives:

1.   Set managers up for success

Although a majority of companies provides general training for managers, far fewer address specifics that are critical to managing teams today, such as how to minimize burnout and ensure promotions are equitable. Research shows that when training focuses on concrete topics like these, it leads to better results. Companies could also benefit from stepping back to make sure people managers have the time and resources they need to their jobs well. Managers have seen their scope of work expand dramatically over the past two years, and, understandably, many are struggling with the added responsibilities.

2.   Hold managers accountable and reward those who excel

While virtually all companies build business goals into managers' performance reviews, very few do the same for metrics related to people management and DEI. This is an incomplete view of performance, but it's relatively easy to fix. It's increasingly common for employees to review their manager's performance, and prompts to gather more expansive input can be added to employee evaluation forms. Many companies track attrition rates, promotion rates, and other career outcomes and conduct surveys to measure employee satisfaction and well- being; insights from these processes can be built into managers' performance evaluations.

In addition, companies can take steps to more clearly signal their expectations and reward results, such as sharing well-being and diversity metrics with all employees and publicly acknowledging managers who stand out for their efforts to support employees and foster inclusion on their teams.

Women in the workplace – Recommendations

A road map to gender equality

To make meaningful and sustainable progress towards gender equality, companies should focus on two broad goals: getting more women into leadership and retaining the women leaders they already have. This will require pushing beyond common practices. Companies that have better representation of women, especially women of color, are going further. They're doubling down on setting goals, tracking outcomes, and holding leaders accountable – the building blocks of driving organizational change. They're offering more specific and actionable training so managers are better equipped to support their teams and employees know how to practice allyship. They're creating dedicated programs to make sure women get the mentorship and sponsorship they deserve. And they're offering a constellation of benefits to improve women's day-to-day work experiences: flexibility, emergency childcare benefits, and mental, health supports. Companies that want to see better results would benefit from following their lead and breaking new ground.

Most companies also need to take specific, highly targeted steps to fix their "broken rung." This starts with identifying where the largest gap in promotions is for women in their pipeline – for a majority of companies, this will be the first step to manage, but it could be at higher levels, too. Then companies need to make sure women and men are put up for promotions at similar rates, monitor outcomes to make sure they're equitable, and root out biased aspect of their evaluation process.

An overview of the policies and programs that drive progress

Based on an analysis of HR and DEI best practices, we have identified three district categories of policies and programs for advancing and retaining women:

- **Table stakes** have been adopted by more than 75 per cent of companies – and while important, they're not driving enough progress on their own.

- **Leading practices** are less common than table stakes – and more prevalent in companies that have a higher representation of women and women of color.

- **Emerging practices** are relatively rare – adopted by less than 30 per cent of all companies – but show promising early results.

To accelerate progress on gender equality, companies should consider adopting more leading and emerging practices – and continues to look for opportunities to break new ground.

How Intuit increased the number of women in tech roles

Between 2018 and 2020, Intuit launched two major initiates designed to grow the representation of women in technical roles – one that helps prospective employees up-skill, the other that eases the on-ramp for employees who've taken career breaks:

- **The Apprenticeship Pathway Program** is a seven month software development program for prospective employees who don't have a computer science degree and have never worked as a technologist. The program is open to people of all genders, but Intuit makes a specific effort to recruit and enroll women and people of color. Apprentices take programming course, work directly on company projects, and receive mentorship from Intuit developers. More than 80 per cent of apprentices are ultimately hired into full-time roles.

- **The "Intuit Again" return to work program** is aimed at tech workers who've taken career breaks, most of whom are women, Participants join an Intuit for 16 weeks, where they receive training to learn new programming languages and work with a dedicated mentor. To date, nearly 70 per cent of Intuit participants have been hired full-time by Intuit.

How Citi exceeded its representatIon goals?

In 2018, Citi set a representation goal of 40 per cent to the assistant vice president – an important target, since women are underrepresented at these levels in banking and consumer finance.

•   **Proactive recruiting**. In 2021, Citi launched a Diversity Sourcing team in the U.S. to identify diverse talent, including women in mid-level and senior-level roles. Citi has also invested in mentorship programs and internship targeting women college graduate to ensure a strong pipeline of women into management roles.

•   **Inclusive hiring practices**. Citi has taken steps to make hiring more inclusive at the assistant vice president and managing director levels, such as using diverse slates and offering inclusivity training for all hiring managers. The training includes guidance for writing inclusive job descriptions, creating diverse slates and interview panels, and for recruiting diverse slates through active outreach.

•   **Developing talented women**. Citi has expanded their "Women's Career Empowerment Program" for early and mid-career women so that it now reaches 14,000 employees worldwide. Women participate in four training sessions over four months, covering strategic communication, decision-making, and networking. The women managers also receive training on how to support the women's career growth.

Women in the workplace – Conclusion

Companies need to hold on to the leaders shaping the future of work

The Covid-19 crisis and racial reckoning of 2020 pushed corporate America to re-imagine the way we work. Two and a half years in, employees don't want to return to the workplace of the past. They want to move forward.

This is especially true for women. Women are ambitious and hardworking. They're more inclusive and empathetic leaders. And they want to work for companies that are prioritizing the cultural changes that are improving work: flexibility, employee well-being, and diversity, equity, and inclusion.

Companies that rise to the moment will attract and retain women leaders – and this will lead to a better workplace for everyone. They'll win war for talent today and into the future.

THE END

9 789355 849717